E BERHARD
A RNOLD

MODERN SPIRITUAL MASTERS
Robert Ellsberg, Series Editor

This series introduces the writing and vision of some of the great spiritual masters of the twentieth century. Along with selections from their writings, each volume includes a comprehensive introduction, presenting the author's life and writings in context and drawing attention to points of special relevance to contemporary spirituality.

Some of these authors found a wide audience in their lifetimes. In other cases recognition has come long after their deaths. Some are rooted in long-established traditions of spirituality. Others charted new, untested paths. In each case, however, the authors in this series have engaged in a spiritual journey shaped by the influences and concerns of our age. Such concerns include the challenges of modern science, religious pluralism, secularism, and the quest for social justice.

At the dawn of a new millennium this series commends these modern spiritual masters, along with the saints and witnesses of previous centuries, as guides and companions to a new generation of seekers.

Already published:
Dietrich Bonhoeffer (edited by Robert Coles)
Simone Weil (edited by Eric O. Springsted)
Henri Nouwen (edited by Robert A. Jonas)
Pierre Teilhard de Chardin (edited by Ursula King)
Charles de Foucauld (edited by Robert Ellsberg)
Oscar Romero (by Marie Dennis, Rennie Golden, and Scott Wright)

Forthcoming volumes include:
Karl Rahner
John Main
Flannery O'Connor
Brother Roger of Taizé

MODERN SPIRITUAL MASTERS SERIES

EBERHARD ARNOLD

*Writings selected
with an Introduction by*

JOHANN CHRISTOPH ARNOLD

ORBIS BOOKS

Maryknoll, New York 10545

The Catholic Foreign Mission Society of America (Maryknoll) recruits and trains people for overseas missionary service. Through Orbis Books, Maryknoll aims to foster the international dialogue that is essential to mission. The books published, however, reflect the opinions of their authors and are not meant to represent the official position of the society.

To obtain more information about Maryknoll and Orbis Books, please visit our website at www.maryknoll.org.

Note to the reader: Apart from the essay "Why We Live in Community," all of the selections in this book were excerpted from much longer pieces and may represent only a small part of the original. The sun-heart emblem that appears under each chapter heading was designed for Eberhard Arnold by an artist friend in Berlin and symbolizes the fiery love that radiates from the heart of God.

Manufactured in the United States of America

Library of Congress Cataloging-in-Publication Data

Arnold, Eberhard, 1883–1935.
  [Selections. English. 2000]
  Eberhard Arnold / writings selected with an introduction by Johann Christoph Arnold.
    p. cm. – (Modern spiritual masters series)
  ISBN 1-57075-304-0 (pbk.)
    1. Hutterian Brethren – Doctrines. 2. Spiritual life – Hutterian Brethren. I. Arnold, Johann Christoph, 1940– II. Title. III. Series.

BX8129.B65 A7218213 2000
289.7′3 – dc21

99-087489

Arnold's significance is not limited to his relatively small community. Some day the whole family of humankind will recognize what Eberhard Arnold means for the spiritual renewal of man in these dark and troubled times. God sent him as a light into the darkness, to show erring man the right way and the true goal.

— PITTER PREMYSL, General Secretary
Christian Communists, Prague, 1935

Contents

Acknowledgments

Even a small book does not come into being without the efforts of many people. Among those who must be thanked especially are the brothers and sisters of the Bruderhof Archives, without whose faithful and loving work my grandfather's words would never have been preserved or translated. I am also indebted to Robert Ellsberg of Orbis Books, whose personal interest inspired this project from the very beginning.

JOHANN CHRISTOPH ARNOLD
July 1999

Introduction

Blessed are they who die in the Lord;
their works follow after them.

Widely sought after as a writer and lecturer in his day, Eberhard Arnold remains largely unknown to modern readers. Small but growing numbers of readers, however, are discovering the relevance of his work, which Thomas Merton said "stirs to repentance and renewal."

Though he was my grandfather, I never met him. He died at fifty-two, five years before I was born, but I feel as though I have always known him — both through my grandmother's radiant memories of their life together and through his heavily underlined books, which my father inherited.

Much more than a writer, philosopher, and theologian, he was loved most of all for his humility, his fatherly friendship, and his deep faith. He was born in 1883 into a long line of academics, but his life was hardly conventional. In a time and place where church and state were anything but separate, he threw away what might have been a brilliant career when he left the state church at age twenty-five. By thirty-seven, he had abandoned middle-class life altogether. He spent his last fifteen years at the Bruderhof (literally, "place of brothers"), the religious community he founded in 1920, but remained active in traveling, lecturing, and writing until his death in 1935.

Little of what he wrote is available to readers today: only a small number of the thousands of talks, essays, and letters he left behind have ever been published in English. In a certain way, however, this would cause him no dismay: especially toward the end of his life, he spoke often of his own inadequacies, pointing instead to the working of the Holy Spirit. And yet his witness, however small, cannot be left unrecognized. His insights into the human condition are as relevant today as they were in the early twenties, and his call to discipleship rings as true now as it did then.

What was his message, and how did he arrive at his radical faith? His own words, spoken in 1933, say it best:

> In my youth, I tried to lead people to Jesus through study-ing the Bible and through lectures, talks, and discussions. But there came a time when I recognized that this was no longer enough. I began to see the tremendous power of mammon, of discord, of hate, and of the sword: the hard boot of the oppressor upon the neck of the oppressed. I saw that dedication to the soul alone did not fulfill all of Jesus' commandments; he wanted us to care for people's bodies as well.
>
> From 1913 to 1917 my wife, Emmy, and I sought pain-fully for an understanding of the truth. Shortly before the outbreak of the war, I had written to a friend saying that I could not go on. I had preached the gospel but felt that I needed to do more. The cause of Jesus was more than just a meeting of individual souls; it had to become a tan-gible, real-life experience! So we searched everywhere: not only in old writings — in the Sermon on the Mount and in other scriptures — but also in books about the working class and their oppression by the economic and social order. We wanted to find the way of Jesus, of Francis of Assisi; the way of the prophets.
>
> The war years brought unforgettable horrors. One young officer came back with both of his legs shot off. He came home to his fiancée, hoping to receive the loving care he needed so badly from her, and she informed him that she had become engaged to a man with a healthy body.
>
> Then the time of hunger came to Berlin. People ate tur-nips morning, noon, and night. And when they turned to the officials for money or food, they were told to eat more turnips. At the same time, well-to-do "Christian" families

in the middle of the city were able to keep cows and had milk! In 1917 I saw a horse fall in the street. The driver was knocked aside by a mob of men who rushed in to cut pieces of meat from its warm body — they had to bring something home to their children and wives! Dead children were carted through the streets wrapped in newspapers; there was neither time nor money for coffins.

It was during this time that I visited a woman in a basement dwelling. Water ran down the walls of her cellar, and the only window in the room was closed because it opened to the street above. She had tuberculosis but could not afford isolation; her relatives lived in the same room with her. I offered to find another dwelling for her, but she refused — she wanted to die where she had always lived. And she was already a corpse!

Gradually it became clear to us that the way of Jesus was practical and tangible. It was more than concern for the soul. It said, very simply: "If you have two coats, give to him who has none. Give food to the hungry, and do not turn away from your neighbor when he needs you. When asked for an hour's work, give two. Strive for justice. If you want to marry and start a family, then see that those around you can do the same. If you seek education and work, make these available to others also. And if it is your duty to care for your own health, then fulfill this duty to others. Treat them as you would treat yourself. Enter through the narrow gate, for it is the only way to the kingdom of God."

We knew that we had to become as poor as beggars — that we, like Jesus, had to take upon ourselves the *whole* need of human beings. We had to hunger for justice more than for water and bread. We knew we would be persecuted for the sake of this justice, but our righteousness would be greater than that of the moralists and theologians. And we would be filled with fire from above: we would receive the Holy Spirit.

But we could not endure the life that we were living any longer.

My grandfather practiced what he preached, and by 1920 he and my grandmother, with five young children, had left their comfortable suburb of Berlin-Steglitz for a dilapidated villa in the Rhön mountains. This move was more than just a geographic relocation; it was a radical change of life. Though the years ahead would be ones of grinding poverty, the Arnolds would never again be held back by financial worry. The Sermon on the Mount was not merely an ideal, but a way to live. From now on their house would be open to the destitute; their lives would be consumed in caring not only for souls but bodies as well.

To their friends, this was madness; to them, it was an "opportunity for love and joy." But rash as it seemed, their move from Berlin — as their earlier move away from the state church — was a step taken in faith; or rather, as my grandmother often said, a leap:

> We had no financial basis of any kind for realizing our dreams of starting a new life. But that made no difference. It was time to turn our backs on the past and start afresh...to burn all our bridges and put our trust entirely in God — like the birds of the air and the flowers of the field. This trust was to be our foundation — the surest foundation, we felt, on which to build.

Eberhard's spiritual quest had already begun years earlier when, as a teenager on summer vacation at the home of his mother's cousin, he had begun to read the New Testament. This relative, a Lutheran pastor who had once sided with local weavers during a labor dispute, impressed him considerably. By the time he returned home, he had become aware that his clothes were better than those of many other classmates, and that when his parents held a party, they invited only their coterie of well-to-do academics — and not the poor of the street. His questions about these matters infuriated his father, but he remained undeterred. Were Jesus' words metaphor only? Sooner or later, he must find out.

In the years to follow he estranged himself from his schoolmates as well: he took his new-found faith so seriously that he sought out former teachers and begged their forgiveness for his previous unruly and dishonest behavior. By the time he was a university student, however, his fervor no longer caused embarrassment: Dwight L. Moody's religious revival was now sweeping Germany, and his enthusiasm for its cause soon gained him popularity as both a writer and speaker.

It was around this time that he first met my grandmother, Emmy von Hollander, known to us children as "Oma." The daughter of a law professor, she shared Eberhard's social and intellectual background and like him was active in the revival movement. Within a month, the two were engaged. They would remain together until his death, twenty-eight years later.

It was during this same time in 1907 that the question of baptism emerged as a central theme. Many young adults felt that their christening had made them heirs to a culture but not a faith, and so began to have themselves rebaptized. Characteristically, Eberhard cautioned Emmy to test everything in prayer. The issues were complex and required careful consideration:

> To me it seems almost certain that baptism of believers is biblical. But the question is complicated, and we must test it slowly and objectively. Let us say nothing until we have reached incontestable clarity. Let us search honestly and thoroughly for the will of God, and then act accordingly. Either way, however, we shall not be moved one millimeter from the center. What we need is Jesus — nothing else!

In the end, thorough study convinced the young couple that the baptism intended by Jesus meant baptism of believing adults, not infants, and both were baptized in 1908.

The consequences were swift: Eberhard was denied the opportunity to sit for his exams in theology, and he was forbidden to meet Emmy for one year. This punishment was painful, but he and Emmy had expected nothing less. Their baptism was a declaration of war against the state church and as such was no small matter — least of all for a young man whose father was professor of church history and whose name was synonymous with good society. As always, however, he exhorted Emmy to persevere in faith:

> This momentous decision will give our life a sharply defined direction, laden with suffering....What will happen only the Lord knows, but that is sufficient. I know with certainty that Jesus will lead us excellently!

The years that followed were tumultuous. Eberhard was forced to change his course of study to philosophy; he wrote his thesis on Nietzsche and earned his doctoral degree in 1909. He and Emmy were married the same year, and their house soon became a gathering place for all kinds of writers, students, and radicals.

War came in 1914, and although Eberhard was called to the front, he was discharged within weeks on account of his tuberculosis. He supported the war effort with nationalistic fervor all the same, publishing propaganda as the newly hired editor of a magazine run by one of his boyhood friends. As the war dragged on, however, he became increasingly disillusioned, and by 1917 he was a convinced pacifist.

Even earlier, his chief concern had been the care of the soul, as this statement on the ultimate goals of his literary work shows:

> The name of our publishing house, *Die Furche* ("furrow"), should be a powerful admonition to inner deepening. A furrow is something that has been plowed up and opened; such an opening must precede every sowing. Only where the plow of God has exposed the inner life can such a sowing bear fruit. A deepening of the inner life can be brought about only by the plowing of repentance — that inner revolution and reevaluation which leads to *metanoia*, a fundamental transformation of mind and heart.

His views were not shared by all, however, and over the next two years it became clear to him that his calling was no longer one with that of the publishing house. By 1919, his insistence that Christ's teachings were meant to be practiced in daily life was causing increasing controversy with the directors of *Die Furche*. Emmy writes:

> There were always tensions at work. Everyone could appreciate the confusion of the youth, a result of the suffering of the war, and then the turmoil of revolution. But while some wanted to lead them back onto the beaten track of pietism, others — Eberhard among them — saw public events with an entirely new eye. They had learned a lesson from the blatant inequalities between rich and poor, from the war psychosis they had so painfully observed. They believed they had to go an entirely different way: the way of Jesus, the way of the Sermon on the Mount.

The years that followed brought widespread social change. In much the same way as American hippies rebelled against the complacent affluence of their parents during the Vietnam War, young people in the Weimar Republic turned their backs on the social conservatism and aristocratic pretensions of the failed Prussian empire.

Thousands of them left the cities for the country, roaming farms and mountains in their search for truth and meaning in life. They lacked no diversity in background and opinion but held in common the belief that old structures and conventions must die and finally give way to something new. And although many of them soon drifted into the hedonism and moral decay that characterized the post-war period, others, like my grandparents, saw in the Youth Movement* an affirmation of their spiritual quest for wholeness.

The Youth Movement sought answers to life's questions in the simplicity of rural life, in the trees and mountains and meadows, and in the poetry and literature of the romantics. They rejected the crass materialism of the cities in favor of the rural life, with its simple pleasures of folk dancing and hiking, and turned their backs on the sterility of factory life to embrace the hard work —

---

*The Free German Youth Movement of the early 1920s, not the Hitler Youth of the mid-1930s.

and the stench — of the farm. For them, the collapse of civilization as they knew it was proof of humankind's need for nature
and for God.

But it was the question of separating the spiritual from the
material that brought about the birth of Sannerz, the religious
community my grandparents founded in 1920. To them, life
could not be lived in fragments. Everything was connected: work
and leisure, family and friends, religion and politics — all these
had to become one. Repentance could not effect change in one
area while leaving another untouched. And if one sphere of life
was to be influenced and molded by God, then all other spheres
must be influenced by God as well.

It was this recognition that led them to leave Berlin for a new
life in the impoverished farming district of Fulda, opening their
doors to wandering musicians, artists, anarchists, and tramps. If
the words of Jesus could be lived out in the first century, they
could be lived out again now; if Christ could pour out his spirit
on earth two thousand years ago, it could happen again today.
Such was their faith as they ventured to create a community of
work and of goods: a life in which everything belonged to all and
yet to none.

This determination to apply the Gospel in practical ways led
to my grandfather's final resignation from *Die Furche* during the
spring of 1920. By June of the same year, he and Oma had moved
into the storage rooms of Gasthaus Lotzenius, an inn in the small
village of Sannerz.

Within weeks, however, my grandfather was publishing again.
He had no money and only a tiny staff, but he felt compelled
to publicize as widely as possible the truths that he and my
grandmother, with the small circle that gathered around them at
Sannerz, had begun to recognize. Formulating his thoughts that
August, he wrote:

> The task and mission of our publishing work is to proclaim
> living renewal, to summon people to the actions of Christ;
> to disseminate the thinking of Jesus in the midst of national
> and social distress; to apply Christianity publicly; to testify

to God's action in present history. It is not a church question — it is a religious question. We must face the deepest forces of Christianity and recognize them as indispensable in the solution of the crucial problems in contemporary culture. With breadth of vision and with energetic daring, our publishing house will steer its course into the torrent of present-day thought. Its work in fields that are apparently religiously neutral will gain for us relationships leading to our greatest tasks in life.

Already at this stage, my grandfather was an established writer. He had numerous books and articles to his name, and definite ideas for even more ambitious projects. Aside from continued lecturing and writing, he planned to publish a series of books devoted to Zinzendorf, Kierkegaard, Augustine, and Dostoyevsky, as well as books on German women mystics, Tertullian, and the Christians of the first and second centuries.

By September, however, his co-editor, Otto Herpel, had resigned, unable to agree to a document stating that the new publishing venture would call only on those writers whose articles were written "in Christ, of Christ, and toward Christ." Eberhard had become "too pietistic," even for his best friends.

He was hardly deterred by these disappointments, however, and plunged even more feverishly into the work of building up Sannerz and the publishing house. As he put it, any apparent defeat in the face of partisan socialism and religious politics was "in actual fact a victory for the decisive spirit of the Sermon on the Mount."

Sannerz grew rapidly over the next two years. Business was relatively good, and dozens of articles, pamphlets, and books were written, edited, and produced. Yet the publishing work was only part of the community's mission. The founders of Sannerz believed strongly that community was the solution to all of life's questions: economic, social, educational, political, and sexual issues were all addressed and fully answered by the common life. Even more, then, the literary achievements of the first years at Sannerz are staggering, considering the interruptions by the two thousand visitors who came in 1921, as well as the farm work and household chores that had to be done.

But the summer of 1922 brought trouble: while traveling in Holland, Eberhard was notified by telephone that the shareholders of his fledgling publishing house had met to liquidate the firm. They accused him of financial irresponsibility, idealism, and even fraud.

The crisis erupted over the management of the community's publishing house. My grandparents had left Sannerz several weeks earlier to visit a sister community in Holland, but while they were gone inflation had suddenly soared, and loans that had not been due for months were suddenly recalled. The community back home at Sannerz panicked, but my grandparents advised inner calm. To them, the words of Jesus about the lilies and the birds were not mere poetry; they were a mandate for the disciple's life.

In the end, a friend surprised them with a large envelope of guilders which, when converted to marks, came to the exact amount due at the bank the next day. Inflation had been on their side and, more importantly, their faith had been rewarded. Too late, however, they returned home to find the publishing venture liquidated — by the very friends they had left in charge.

More than forty people left Sannerz in the following weeks, all firmly convinced that spiritual and temporal matters could not and should not be mixed. The "experiment" was over: people were too weak, too human, too selfish to live by faith. Yet for my grandparents, Sannerz had been no experiment: it was a calling, and they would hold fast to it.

Within weeks, there was a complete split between those to whom faith was merely an ideal and those to whom it was a living reality that had to determine every decision and every action.

In addition to splitting the circle at Sannerz, those who left also divided the publishing house. They took with them both office equipment and several best-selling titles, including the periodical, which they began to put out under a new name only months later.

The crisis was especially painful because of the bitter and slanderous accusations with which so many people left Sannerz. But as a shareholder admitted during the liquidation proceedings in August, Eberhard had done nothing dishonest. It was simply a matter of faith versus economic considerations: "What separates Eberhard Arnold from the rest of us is his conviction that faith must determine *all* relationships, including financial ones."

Years later, a Vienna newspaper would agree, stating that Eberhard Arnold was one of the very few publishers who not only published religious works, but dared to apply their message in his own life. This was the heart of his vision. The spiritual had to penetrate and transform the material, for Christ intended not only words but deeds: "Be doers of the word, and not hearers only."

Thus my grandparents rejected the notion that their community was an escape, that they had isolated themselves from the problems of society. True, the people who joined Sannerz had removed themselves from the mainstream of modern life, but only to the extent that they could live unfettered by it. Their ultimate goal was to remain a corrective in a world that had gone badly awry: to be, in the words of Jesus, salt and light.

Yet my grandfather never saw himself as unique or capable. His discipleship was uncompromising, but never self-satisfied; he saw himself as nothing other than the servant of a higher cause. He always sought out the truth in others. And he saw the community he guided not as a lifestyle or institution, but as a free-flowing movement that was driven by — and that would die without — the wind of the Holy Spirit. Looking back on the first years at Sannerz, he later said:

At that time none of us was so narrow-minded as to fail to appreciate the work of God in other people and in other spiritual movements. Perhaps our danger was rather in the opposite direction — that for some time we held back from expressing certain insights into God's ultimate truth, in order to avoid putting pressure on people who had not yet been awakened or called.

We were certain that these people had been struck by God — that they were in the midst of a mighty movement of heart. But they had not yet fully grasped what God wanted in the shaking of their souls, and so we spoke with them only about those things which moved them at that moment. We did not force on them things to which their hearts had not yet opened.

So it was that many spiritual movements came to us. And we were not such foolish missionaries as to say that Buddhism was of the devil or Lao-tse the Antichrist. We recognized God's Spirit at work in Buddha and Lao-tse. And because we recognized this, we ourselves were animated by what they brought to us from God — even if they spoke in strange tongues.

Thus we did not speak of mission in the sense of going out to people. There was so much life in the house, so much coming and going, that we were a mission station already, in the midst of heathen Germany. But it was never that we were the converters and the others the ones to be converted. Rather, we recognized the Holy Spirit at work.

The rooms at Sannerz were filled with a power that did not come from us, nor from those who visited us. It was a power that came from God. People brought it with them, and they in turn felt it in us. But neither they nor we possessed this power; rather, it surrounded us like an invisible fluid, like the wind of the Spirit that visited the waiting apostles at Pentecost.

This power did not adhere to particular people. It could not be possessed or held fast, or used for gain or profit. It was an event, a happening, an occurrence; it was history. It was a manifestation of the eternal and everlasting in time and space. It was a communication with a primal force, which we could never have explained in a human or logical way. That was the secret of those times. There was something at work that was more than psychic, something that could not be explained in terms of emotions. It was something spiritual, something of the Holy Spirit.

But we never thought then — it would have seemed a kind of craziness to us! — that only people like us, or even just the handful of people at Sannerz, were visited by God's Spirit or were illuminated by the Spirit of Christ. To the contrary, we felt the blowing of the Spirit in all people and all places. The important thing for us was to feel this breath of God and to recognize it.

We ourselves had to live according to the calling that had come to us from the words and life of Jesus, from the prophetic image of God's future kingdom. We had to be true to this calling to the end. We believed we could best serve all those who were touched by the breath of God by living out the reality of our ultimate cause: the objectivity of God's will, and the content and character of his kingdom.

We were called nature lovers — people said that we wanted to go "back to nature" — but that is not at all what we wanted. To the contrary, we looked beyond nature itself and to the divine at work within it. The greatest thing in our movement was that the Creator was honored in his creation. We were not sun-worshipers, but we had an inner feeling for the symbolism of the sun and for the kind of Creator who must have created it. . . .

It may seem strange that such an insignificant group could experience such lofty feelings of peace and community, but it was so. It was a gift from God. And only one antipathy was bound up in our love: a rejection of the systems of civilization; a hatred of the falsities of social stratification; an antagonism to the spirit of impurity; an opposition to the moral coercion of the clergy. The fight that we took up was a fight against these alien spirits. It was a fight for the Spirit of God and Jesus Christ.

By 1931, however, the movement of heart that had swept Germany only a decade earlier had all but dried up. So my grandfather looked farther afield, visiting the Hutterites of Canada and the midwestern United States. Rooted in sixteenth-century Moravia, this group still lived in small communities, sharing all things in common. They were perhaps too narrow-minded and dogmatic for his liking, but they nevertheless represented the

purest form of communal Christianity he had ever met. And so
he joined hands with their four-hundred-year-old movement after
a year of careful consideration.

He had immediately recognized the danger of their conser-
vative pietism, but emphasized that he was attracted not to
twentieth-century Hutterianism but to the Hutterianism of the
sixteenth century, that movement of faith that had left behind
thousands of martyrs. Also, he had never wanted to found his
own sect but again and again sought to join with like-minded
groups. And by 1931 he somehow sensed that he would not live
much longer. He had seen numerous community attempts collapse and had been amazed to find that the Hutterites were still
living in community after four hundred years. Joining them, he
felt, was a safeguard for the Bruderhof.

Of his experiences in North America, he wrote:

> In spite of their weaknesses, which I have openly brought
> to light, these American communities have kept from their
> sixteenth-century origins a spiritual vitality — a creativity
> in working and organizing along communal lines — that
> comes from the Holy Spirit....
>
> My overall impression is that the community life of these
> thirty-five hundred souls is something overpoweringly great.
> Their spirit of community is genuine, pure, clear, and deep.
> There is nothing in the whole world, neither in books and
> writings, nor in any other present-day groups, that can
> be compared to the essence, character, and spirit of their
> brotherhood....
>
> Though in full recognition of our own origins, inspired
> by the Youth Movement and by the Sermon on the Mount,
> I have decided to join forces with them. The question of
> financial support is of a secondary nature.

Despite my grandfather's enthusiastic adoption of early Anabaptist spirituality, however, his hopes for a close economic
relationship with the North American Hutterites never materi-
alized, because of both the great distance between Germany and
Canada and his untimely death.

The first of two Gestapo raids occurred in 1933. Eberhard was not intimidated, however, and sent off reams of documents to the local Nazi officials, explaining his vision of a Germany under God. Before his death in 1935 he would write even to Hitler, urging him to renounce the ideals of National Socialism and to work instead for God's kingdom — and sending him a copy of his book *Innerland*. Not surprisingly, this letter was never answered. Later, the entire community was exiled to England and Liechtenstein; remarkably, not a single member was deported to a concentration camp.

My grandfather's death came suddenly in 1935, the result of complications following the amputation of a gangrenous leg. But as his friend the scholar Hermann Buddensieg wrote years later, he is still very much alive today:

> Do not be surprised that I talk with you as if you were still right with me. For what does the present know of what is yonder? You are not dead; no, you are alive in the Spirit....
>
> And now we are together again, my friend, at Sannerz, in the Rhön, and in my study on the banks of the Neckar.
>
> The people come and go, young and old, looking for refuge in their need. They are wrapped up in themselves, unnatural, cramped and stiffened, exaggerated, without a goal beyond themselves. And yet your house has an open door; no one is first asked who he is....
>
> We work in the fields and in the house. Together we toil for an understanding of the people and events around us. I see the roguish glint in your eyes, your mischievous smile and waggish beard, your cheerful laugh when the peculiarities of human life force themselves upon us. We are often wearied with dull, commonplace talk, but we also laugh freely and heartily, in gales of truly Homeric laughter....
>
> That was your gift. Your wit was pithy, but free of poisonous hypocrisy. You had no love for stuffiness or sweetness. About you there was no penetrating smell of "Christianity," no cliquishness, no sentimentality. To seek out heretics was just as foreign to you as was the addiction

to straighten out everyone according to your own way. You valued other people as long as they were earnest, and you came to terms with the insincere. You found a way with the most pigheaded peasant and with the most stubborn "man of God." You were a brother to them when they needed you, and your manner was at all times cheerful, genuinely animated by trust.

You lived life from the center and from the depths. You did not inherit Christ from others, but from out of your own inner experience and encounter. You were one who was truly freed by Christ, who was changed by him. You were free of anxiety. Your faith was no mere acceptance of truths, no flight of fear, but certainty. And therefore there was nothing of conventional Christianity in you, for you knew precisely that Christ was no "Christian."

You opposed all appearance, all posturing, and all self-righteousness. You were not concerned with dogma, but rather with the life of Christ, with the community of brothers and sisters in the sense of the primitive church.

You took humanity for what it is. You were as distant from illusion as from misunderstanding. You knew demonic powers and the weight of the age, but these things came to you not in isolated recognition, but as a binding call to help your brothers.

You knew the power of the church community within the great current of a completely different world. But you never recruited. Whoever was called, heard, and thus came to you; some to live with you and your friends in community; others, touched by your insight, to remain as good friends....

Let me embrace you, my friend! You are present — a witness of the new life in Christ; a man of kindness, a friend of freedom, a brother of knowing love, but yet one of such decisiveness that you discern and separate spirits.

There is no doubt that Eberhard would have disapproved of this eloquent eulogy, and thus it is fitting that this introduction end with words he spoke on his fiftieth birthday, in July 1933. Here he is no longer just my grandfather, but a man of God, a prophetic voice in a world that needs him now more than then:

> On this day I have been especially conscious of my lack of ability, of how unsuited my own nature is to the work I have been given. I have remembered how God called me when I was only sixteen, and how I have stood in his way — with the result that so much of what he wanted to do has been left unfinished. It remains a miracle nevertheless that his work has been revealed and testified to in us feeble human beings — not through our merits, but because we have been accepted again and again through the grace of Jesus and his forgiveness of sins.
>
> I have had to think of Hermas, that early Christian writer who describes the building of the great temple — how he refers to the many stones that must be thrown away. The masons try to use them, but if they do not fit, even after their corners have been chiseled down, then they must be thrown away — as far away as possible. And even the stones that are used must first be chiseled very sharply before they can be set into the wall....
>
> What concerns me most of all is the powerlessness of human beings, even of the person who has been entrusted with some task. Only God is mighty; we are completely powerless. Even for the work that has been given us, we are wholly without power. We cannot fit a single stone into the church community. We can provide no protection whatsoever for the community when it has been built up. We cannot even devote anything to the cause by our own power. We are completely without power. But just this is why God has called us: because we know we are powerless.
>
> It is hard to describe how our own power must be stripped off us, how our own power must be dropped, dismantled, torn down, and put away. But it must happen, and it will not happen easily, nor through any single heroic decision. Rather, it must be done in us by God.

This is the root of grace: the dismantling of our own power. Only to the degree that our own power is dismantled will God give us his Spirit. If a little power of our own rises up among us, the Spirit and authority of God retreats in the same moment and to the corresponding degree. This is the single most important insight regarding the kingdom of God....

The Holy Spirit produces effects that are deadly for the old life and that at the same time have a wakening and rousing power for the new. So let us use this day to give glory to God. Let us pledge to him the dismantling of our own power. Let us declare our dependence upon grace.

1

God's Revolution

A CALL TO THE INNER LIFE

Despite the negative connotations the word may imply, "revolution" comes closest to describing the spiritual upheaval to which Arnold calls us. The following address was delivered in November 1917, but its message is not dated: the need for inner renewal in the face of overwhelming social and political change is as vital today as it was then. And Arnold's assertion that Bolshevism would fail to bring about peace and justice is prophetic. Certainly, the outer life has to change. But the inner life has to change first, and this change can come about only through repentance.

There is much talk today about upheaval, and in fact, we all feel that we are in the midst of the greatest upheaval humankind can experience. As a result of the war, our European civilization is undergoing a tremendous change. It is a change that brings judgment and chastisement from God over all that we thought we had so firmly under our control, and it has cast us down from the heights of presumption and pride.

The greatest changes are taking place in the economic sphere. A powerful wave of social upheaval has swept across Russia, a wave which has not yet run its course. We have no idea what kinds of change will still take place there in the distribution of

wealth between rich and poor, in industry and commerce, in buying and selling. We cannot yet foresee how far the revolution
in outward things will affect everything else. But one thing is
certain: we need an upheaval.

Certainly most people will get no further than applying it to
outward matters. They are like the Social Democrat who stated,
"We have no time to spend on inner matters, for the outer ones
keep us busy enough." And that is the danger for most people:
because of their many cares they forget the innermost things and
neglect them, and attend only to outward matters. This is perhaps the worst thing about the pressing circumstances of the
present moment: those who long for change completely overlook
the inner side of life. Yet we must understand that any lasting
change will have to start in the inner life.

What is great in our eyes is an abomination to God. We have
preferred human honor to God's honor, and since we have raised
ourselves up instead of bowing down before God, we have sunk
deeply into sin and death. That is why we need an upheaval: a
complete reversal, a re-valuation of all things and all values.

We proclaim Christ as divine power. Jesus is the Spirit, and
where the Spirit is, there is freedom. Whoever comes under the
influence of this Spirit experiences an upheaval from within, and
this upheaval of the soul brings the renewal that we thirst for and
need. Power from above transforms us from within and makes us
capable of what we would otherwise be quite incapable of. We no
longer live according to the flesh but according to the Spirit. Paul
speaks of this when he says: "If anyone is in Christ, he is a new
creation; the old has passed away. Everything has become new."

Laying aside the old nature and putting on the new is the only
thing that can help us in these times. It is a matter of the Spirit —
a matter of the rule of spirits. Outward things do not matter. It
is the inner things that have power, because behind all outward
powers stand spiritual forces. So if we ask ourselves in what direction our lives should proceed, then there is only one question
that matters. Which spirit will rule over us — the spirit of the
world or the Spirit of God? We face the great either/or: God or
the devil, Christ or Satan.

Jesus is the only one who can effect a change in us — Jesus, who lived among us and who uncovered and unmasked our hypocrisy. Only he can change and transform all things. But we can come under his rulership, under the authority of his Spirit, only through the great upheaval of repentance.

The new birth of which he spoke to Nicodemus, the old man who came to him in the night, is repentance. And repentance is a complete revolution of life. It is conversion from the spirit of darkness to the spirit of light, redemption from all constraints and servitude, from all error and delusion. But we should not worry about how this revolution will penetrate the cultural and political life before we ourselves arrive at it quite personally.

Either we live in sin and remain in sin or we are saved from sin and, through the Spirit of Jesus, die to sin and declare war on sin. For whoever is born of God does not live continually in a condition of sin. He is raised up into God's world of light, into the Spirit's world of power. He is morally renewed and has turned toward God in everything. He is awakened to a fresh and joyful life.

When Jesus proclaimed repentance, he used the word in a way that conveys action. And since Jesus added nothing else to this word but proclaimed it as a single totality, he showed us that it is a deed of entirety. There is no repentance if it is not the repentance of the whole person. There is no repentance if it is not repentance in all departments of life. There is no repentance that does not embrace the whole person, starting from the innermost being and pressing outward into all other spheres.

Repentance must start in the thought-life. Thoughts are giants that produce deeds, and if repentance has not taken place in the depths of our heart and mind, we will never be able to prove it in deeds. But when the life of self is overcome within us, through the divine life of Jesus, then there will be a complete transformation of the outer life. A total change will take place in our dealings with other people, and we will place our former friends before the same decision. If they do not accept repentance, we can no longer be at one with them.

Our repentance will stand the test in our professional lives, in

our concept of duty and of work. We will flee from everything
to do with Satan: the lusts of youth, the love of money, and the
rulership of mammon. Our reading, our leisure, our political activity, and our work will all be placed under the influence of the
Holy Spirit.

Repentance as upheaval! If anyone is in Christ, then that person is a new creature. The old has passed away, and everything
has become new.

•

The great agitation in the world of today makes it more and
more urgent to gain inner strength in those quiet encounters with
Christ that make it possible for us to remain under his rule and
authority. Situated as we are in the midst of a world that is so
terribly unpeaceful, we need constant nourishment for our inner
life. It is important to look beyond confining externals.... Instead
of following the alien spirits of hatred and violence, of lying, impure, and greedy possessiveness, we must follow the one spirit
who alone is stronger than all other spirits....

Without a rebirth in our hearts, we will glean from fluctuating
world events either a false meaning — based on material considerations or on emotional or racial ties — or no meaning at all.
The course of history is interpreted falsely by very many, in the
interests of their own nation or society. For most people, though,
it never has any meaning at all. There is only one possible way
of bringing this confusion to an end: the whole person, for the
whole of life, must undergo a complete about-face toward the
kingdom of God.

Rebirth is the only name we can give to such a radical
change — a change to the complete opposite of our former life.
Only through such a complete change can we see in all that happens the approach and intervention of God's rule. We can never
see the kingdom of God, or have any part in it, without a rebirth
of heart, without breaking down the whole structure of our life
and then making a completely new start. Only a new beginning
that proceeds from the very bottom, a rebirth that goes back to

the root, can prepare us for the kingdom of God. We need a new foundation for our entire personal life.

If we want to avoid suffering inward shipwreck in the storm of public opinion and chaos, then our hidden inner being needs daily the quiet haven of communion with God.

— Innerland

GOD'S REVOLUTION

"Revolution" was a catchword in the upheaval of post–World War I Germany, and Arnold took it as one of his favorite themes. "World Revolution and World Redemption" appeared first in May 1919, and by 1921 there were two more lectures of the same name. All of his life, he decried modern theology's emphasis on "otherness" as opposed to social responsibility. But Arnold was no Marxist, nor even a socialist. Together with Nikolai Berdyaev, the Russian philosopher and theologian, he maintained that the social problems of society could not be solved apart from the spiritual ones, that without a Christ-centered renewal, the ideals of socialism were destined to fail. This article, published in 1926, is typical: it hails not to Lenin, but to the cross.

A radical social revolution, a turning upside down of all relationships and all things in the cause of God's justice, is something we can talk about only when we feel wholeheartedly that this revolution is meant for all people.

All of us need to be turned upside down. We are all guilty of the injustices in our society and the degrading of others in personal and public relationships. And only when we dare to face this corruption squarely can any upheaval begin within us.

In the end, this revolution does not center around the oppressed, who also must be raised up to a genuine life. No, the aim of this decisive battle is essentially greater. It grasps at the root of hostility to life, of mortal sin against life, in every single human being and in public life as a whole.

God's revolution leads toward a community of justice and of

goods that produces new life-values in the material and physical world just as much as in the development of character. It is ever-lasting and without end; it has in its view the origin of life, which lies in eternity and infinity. Its purpose and goal is the ultimate, eternal, and all-encompassing future.

We, however, are limited and restricted. We are short-lived and weak. We are base, and again and again we represent our own mortal interests. Because of this, it is evident that God's revolution can never be realized completely by people such as we are. Therefore the weapon we must choose is faith in the beginning of a new life, the weapon of the Spirit itself.

We must carry on the battle without judging or punishing our fellow human beings and without injuring them. Our attitude to life, and the way we work, must correspond absolutely to the purity of the prophetic Spirit, to the nature of the Eternal and Infinite, to the spirit of our ultimate calling. Only in this way will our authority be effective at all times. And we must allow this revolution to begin over and over and always more profoundly within ourselves. All of us are called to revolution, because all of us are guilty.

Only the creative Power itself can usher in the New Day. After the long day of the dinosaurs, those gigantic dragons of prehistoric times, a new day dawned. In just the same way, after the present time of degenerate and sinful human beings, the Son of Man must dawn, ushered in by a revolution such as the world has never seen. But we cannot comprehend the dawn of this New Day unless we understand the witness of the prophets and the apostles.

Prophecy bears witness against all that is self-seeking, murderous, and antisocial; against all crime against life and community; against all gain through injury to another; against luxury and af-fluence at the expense of those who suffer want; against violence and war.

Prophecy is the most positive witness to love: to the sharing of bread, roof, and clothes with all who are hungry, homeless, and ill-clad; to the release of all people from chains, servitude, and imprisonment; to open hospitality for all wanderers and travelers; to the uprooting of the old and the planting of the new. Prophecy witnesses to the heart's purification from injustice and egocentric limitations; to forgiveness and the removal of evil; to a new heart; to the unconditional dictatorship of the Holy Spirit and the reign of Christ.

The Prophet believes in the realization of the impossible through God. He is a fighter and spokesman for God's goal, and God's future is his present strength. He speaks and acts in it and is ready to lay down his life for it. His goal is unity in God: the unity of the Spirit that gives life and breath to everything. Instead of the coercive state, he seeks the unified, all-fulfilling, and all-guiding Spirit of true community.

This Spirit was the very breath of life for the first Christians. To them, property was rooted in sin. Thus every storeroom and fund belonged to the poor. They saw it as their duty to uncover and to overcome distress, to search out and relieve poverty street by street. Their life was one of utmost simplicity, and their leaders lived like the poorest.

This attack on property as the legal foundation of economic order was consistent with the life-and-death struggle of the early church against the state's pretensions to absolute authority. The rejection of any high public office invested with judiciary power, the refusal to pass judgment on life or death or civic rights, the refusal to carry out orders to kill whether imposed by the law or the military — this rejection applied also to the highest government office, that of emperor. With this attitude, in spite of all their works of love, the first Christians remained everywhere "aliens" and "foreigners" within their society, citizens and ambassadors of a coming supra-political order.

This revolution of faith had its roots in the certainty that every single individual, and even earth's whole atmosphere and the whole of public life, would be freed from the rule of evil and taken possession of by God. In the same way today, the certainty that the New Day is drawing near calls us to a revolution that turns everything upside down. Just now, when most people have chosen a patient acceptance of evolution, when people have resigned and adapted themselves to the fact of degenerate reality, the call to the tragic way of the cross must be heard again.

•

It is not possible to equate a life in Christ, lived by grace, with political socialism. On the other hand I feel strongly that many of the demands of conscience raised by socialists are born of the same longings that animated people in the time of John the Baptist. . . .

The movement of conscience that is alive in socialism and communism is directed against the rule of mammon and bloodshed, against class hatred and greed. This movement comes from deep within; it is a movement of God. But this does not prevent me from recognizing, at the same time, the presence of powerful satanic and demonic forces at work in these same political movements.

What we need today — and what none of us has yet attained — is a simple discipleship of Jesus that responds to the longing of the present but goes beyond spiritually edifying experiences.

— Letter to Friedrich Böhm, 1920

AGAINST BLOODSHED AND VIOLENCE

"Against Bloodshed and Violence" was published in Arnold's magazine, Das neue Werk, *in April 1921. Although he had supported the war effort with nationalistic fervor prior to 1917, Arnold was by this time clearly convinced that reconciliation was not only to be preached, but lived. His premise is straightforward: God's kingdom cannot remain a future ideal, but must become present reality. The character of the present-day church must therefore be in accordance with God's future plan. It follows that the church cannot condone or support violence of any kind.*

Again and again in the life of a nation, and in the class struggle for existence, pent-up tensions and conflicts erupt in violent outbursts. These outbursts reveal exploitation and oppression and the savage instincts of covetous passion. People respond in different ways to this violence: some try to uphold law and order by murderous means, while others feel called to fight for social justice with the oppressed. As Christians, however, we must look further ahead.

Christ witnessed to life, to the unfolding of love, to the unity of all members in one body. He revealed to us the heart of his Father, who lets his sun shine on the wicked as well as the good. He commissioned us to serve life and to build it up, not to tear it down or destroy it. Thus we believe in a future of love and constructive fellowship — in the peace of God's kingdom. And our faith in this kingdom is much more than any wishful longing for the future. Rather, it is a firm belief that God will give us his heart and spirit now, on this earth.

As the hidden, living seed of the future, the church has been entrusted with the spirit of this coming kingdom. Its present character must therefore show now the same peace and joy and justice that it will embody in the future. For this reason, we must speak up in protest against every instance of bloodshed and violence, no matter what its origin.

Our witness and will for peace, for love at any cost, even our own lives, has never been more necessary. Those who tell us that the questions of nonviolence and conscientious objection are no longer relevant are wrong. Just now, these questions are more relevant than ever. But answering them requires courage and perseverance in love.

Jesus knew he would never conquer the spirit of the world with violence, but only by love. This is why he overcame the temptation to seize power over the kingdoms of the earth, and why he speaks of those who are strong in love — the peacemakers — as those who will inherit the land and possess the earth. This attitude was represented and proclaimed strongly by the first Christians, who felt that war and the military profession were irreconcilable with their calling. It is regrettable that serious-minded Christians today do not have the same clear witness.

We acknowledge the existence of evil and sin, but we know it will never triumph. We believe in God and the rebirth of human-kind. And our faith is not faith in evolution, in the inevitable ascent to greater perfection, but faith in the spirit of Christ, faith in the rebirth of individuals and in the fellowship of the church. This faith sees war and revolution as necessary judgment on a de-praved and degenerate world. Faith expects everything from God, and it does not shy away from the collision of spiritual forces. Rather, it longs for confrontation, because the end must come — and after it, a completely new world.

•

I really believe that much good is being said and done in the cause of peace and for the uniting of nations. But I don't think it is enough. If people feel urged to try to prevent or postpone another major European war, we can only rejoice. But what troubles us is whether they will have much success in opposing the war spirit that exists right now:

When over a thousand of our German people have been killed by Hitler — without a trial — isn't that war?

When hundreds of thousands of people in concentration camps are robbed of their freedom and stripped of all dignity, isn't that war?

When hundreds of thousands are sent to Siberia and freeze to death while felling trees, isn't that war?

When in China and Russia millions of people starve to death while in Argentina and other countries millions of tons of wheat are stockpiled, isn't that war?

When thousands of women prostitute their bodies and ruin their lives for the sake of money, isn't that war?

When millions of babies are murdered by abortion each year, isn't that war?

When people are forced to work like slaves because they cannot otherwise feed their children, isn't that war?

When the wealthy live in villas surrounded by parks while other families don't even have a single room to themselves, isn't that war?

When some people build up enormous bank accounts while others earn scarcely enough for basic necessities, isn't that war?

When automobiles, driven at speeds agreeable to their owners, kill sixty thousand people a year in the United States, isn't that war?

—Talk, August 1934

•

We do not represent the pacifism that believes it can prevent future war. This claim is not valid; there is war right up to the present day.

We do not advocate the pacifism that believes in the elimination of war through the restraining influence of certain superior nations.

We do not support the armed forces of the League of Nations, which are supposed to keep unruly nations in check.

We do not agree with a pacifism that ignores the root causes of war — property and capitalism — and tries to bring about peace in the midst of social injustice.

We do not agree with a pacifism that continues fighting while it drafts peace treaties.

We have no faith in the pacifism held by businessmen who beat down their competitors, nor do we believe in the pacifism of people who cannot even live in peace with their own wives.

We reject any pacifism that brings benefits or advantages to certain nations or businesses.

Since there are so many kinds of pacifism we cannot believe in, we would rather not use the word "pacifism" at all. But we are friends of peace, and we want to help bring about peace. Jesus said, "Blessed are the peacemakers!" And if we really want peace, we must represent it in all areas of life. We cannot injure love in any way or for any reason. So we cannot kill anyone; we cannot harm anyone economically; we cannot take part in a system that establishes lower standards of living for manual workers than for academics.

—Talk, August 1934

•

God is our future, even as he is our origin. He approaches us
with a demand and a promise: Break new ground! Away with
what is old and petrified! Become flesh and blood, stirred with
life and feeling! Let the Spirit come over you as rain comes over
the desert, cracked and fissured in its hardness. Let the Spirit
who is God himself enter into you, or you will remain dead
bones!

But what good is religious exercise, what good is worship and
song, if God's will is not done, if our hands are stained with
blood? What good is belief by the unjust, or the confession to
God by those who turn their backs on dying children? Change
completely! Become different; become human! Believe God, and
give your life to God.

This is the message of all the prophets, including John the Baptist: Change radically! Let everything be turned upside down! The
new order is coming. That which now rules the world will be
abolished. Something utterly different will come to this world.
The rulership of God is near!

Jesus did not believe in a god who brings unhappiness, death
and demons, crime and injustice. On the contrary, he proclaims
the God who eliminates all these things. He knows that evil pre-
vails in this world. But he knows more: that it will be overcome,
that everything will become new and different.

This victory over evil is the sole task of Jesus' life. The purpose
of his mission is to overthrow Satan, the tyrant of the earth, to
strip him of power, to occupy his land, to destroy his achievements and works. Jesus promises the most radical new order of
all things, including things political and social, cultural and agri-
cultural, ethnographical and geographical. A new order for all
things — this is the substance of his words.

His will is always one thing: that God's will become history
on earth as it is in heaven, that God, who until now has been
blasphemed, might at last be honored. He wants God's rulership
and harmony, which already governs the circling of the stars and
the laws of matter, to prevail among human beings. That heaven

come to earth — that the earth itself become the kingdom of heaven — that is his goal.

All of Jesus' parables about the kingdom of heaven point to this goal. Think of the ruler who goes away on a journey: he first hands his realm over to his co-workers, entrusting to each certain duties and responsibilities. When he comes back, he calls them together and celebrates joyfully with those who have fulfilled their obligations. In the same way, God entrusts the earth to us until his return.

—Lecture, Saxony, 1924

•

Arnold was revolutionary not only in principle, but in practice — and down to the smallest details. His colleagues were horrified when he discarded his business suit for the tunic and knee britches sported by young radicals, but they were even more shocked when he and his wife, Emmy, decided to exchange their middle-class existence for a life of voluntary poverty. Emmy writes:

We had no financial basis of any kind, either for starting a new business or for buying the villa at Sannerz to use as a community house. But that made no difference. It was time to turn our backs on the past and start afresh in full trust. Well-meaning friends shook their heads: What rash irresponsibility — and five small children at that! Frau Michaelis, the wife of the former Reich-Chancellor, even offered to care for me and the children in the event that Eberhard would really take such an "unusual" step. But after talking with me, she reported to a mutual friend: "She is even more fanatical than he is! There is nothing we can do."

2

The New Justice

Arnold's life-long preoccupation with the Sermon on the Mount was as practical as it was profound. Thus his writings about these words of Jesus have nothing to do with interpretation or analysis. Instead, they point to simple obedience and to a manner of living apart from which we cannot call ourselves Christian.

NOT A NEW LAW

How do we respond to the Sermon on the Mount? The Sermon on the Mount is the first step on the way of discipleship, and as such we must consider it deeply. If we fully grasp the Sermon on the Mount and believe it, then nothing can frighten us — neither our own self-recognition, nor financial threats, nor our own personal weaknesses.

And the Sermon on the Mount is not high-tension moralism, but the revelation of God's power in human life. If we truly surrender to God and allow him to enter our lives, then we will be able to live the new life. But if, like the Tolstoyans, we see the Sermon on the Mount as five new commandments, we will fall right into a trap. For Leo Tolstoy interprets these commandments of Jesus as five new laws: peacefulness with others, sexual purity and marital faithfulness, the refusal to swear oaths, nonresistance to evil, and love of one's enemies. But Jesus did not make new laws; rather, he sharpened the clarity and demands of the old. And the things he touched on are only examples that reveal the powerful effect of God's work; he could have used five hundred or five thousand.

His righteousness is better than anything scholars or theologians can offer. It is something absolutely different; it does not depend on moral intention. It can be fulfilled only through a new way of living: through the life from God that flares up like light, that sears and purifies like salt, that pulses like sap through a tree. It is life, life, life!

—Address, October 1935

•

The Sermon on the Mount reveals Jesus' heart and confronts us with his will. He knows that all are poor and empty, but he will bring happiness and wealth to those who — because they feel their poverty — are open to what he gives. His sermon is not a law, nor does it require any moral effort or exertion of energy. It requires only emptiness, a vacuum of utter spiritual poverty.

In Luke this is written without qualification: Happy are you poor! Blessed are you who hunger and thirst! Blessed are you who weep! Blessed are you who are persecuted! Here there is no hint of a specialized religious life. Rather, the citizens of the kingdom are marked by their poverty and by the fact that they are despised and maligned, that they hunger and thirst and know suffering.

Luke goes on: Woe to you who are rich! Woe to you who are full! Woe to you who laugh! Woe to you who are praised by men! And this "Woe!" applies to all who hang on to their possessions, no matter how admirable or necessary. The prerequisite for the kingdom is poverty. This poverty is not only poverty of material things, but also poverty of spirit, and emptiness of religion and moral wisdom, a mourning for the world and for ourselves, for collective and individual guilt, for material need and for the deepest need of the soul.

The persecution and contempt that must come to those who are poor in this sense will be a persecution for the sake of the new justice. This justice will be hated most of all by those who feel righteous in their wealth and moral rectitude, because it condemns to death their present life on earth.

The nature of this new justice is at the heart of Jesus' teaching. It is blissfulness in poverty. It is the mystery of the changed heart, that radical change proclaimed by John, the last prophet of the first Judaism. He foretold the new order of things envisioned by all the prophets before him, and he proclaimed God as joy and justice and fellowship for all people. Jesus himself was immersed in this future justice, which is God himself.

The entire Sermon on the Mount shows this new justice to be a gift of God. Thus it cannot coexist with the goodness and achievement of people. It appeared only once, in the Son of Man, in Jesus. But it is present today in the risen Lord, active in his spirit, working as the power of the creator, the God of resurrection. The Sermon shows us, then, the character of Jesus himself and therefore the character of his kingdom, which tolerates no awareness of human goodness or nobility, no standing on rights, and no strife between people. Only those who recognize their dependence on God, and who have reverence before God, can understand this.

Becoming a new person in Christ has nothing to do with human effort. Jesus does not say that we *should* be salt or light. Rather, he knows that new birth comes from God. Thus he says we *are* salt and light. But unless salt is salty, it is fit only to be thrown out. And unless light burns and shines and warms, it is not light. Light, like salt, does its task by consuming itself. Love as selfless devotion is the essence of Jesus and his kingdom.

Only out of such love can any fellowship arise. To try to manufacture communal life is just as impossible as to produce a tree in a factory. The building up of community is always the work of God and does not depend on human striving. Creation's law of growth and life stands in contrast to human works, just as the law of the spirit of life is contrasted with the law of sin and death in Paul's Letter to the Romans.

What we cannot accomplish, God can. God's creative spirit governs the law of life, for God is a God of all that is living, not a God of death. The resurrection of Jesus is the ultimate revelation of this law. The Sermon on the Mount can be grasped only where he is proven powerfully to be the Son of God. Otherwise, it remains an impossibility, a utopia or fantasy, self-deception or madness.

The life that springs from the Spirit is like a seed: it must be buried in the soil to die, but then bursts forth bearing fruit. It is the mortal enemy of death and hatred, murder and human effort. Liberating love is life's only fulfillment. Only the love of God can lift us above our human sphere to affirm life and bestow its gifts on all that is living. And God sends his sun on all: on sinners and moralists, on the just and the unjust, on those who seek him and those who blaspheme him. His justice is far removed from that of the moralists and theologians, who emphasize boundaries and differences.

God's heart is mercy. His love goes out to all. He wants justice in external things as much as he wants to shower us with mercy. Thus Luke summarizes the attitude of the citizens of the kingdom with the simple words: Love! Be merciful! Hold on to nothing for yourselves. Do not judge or seek faults in others. Give to all and be generous to your enemies!

The way of reconciliation and nonresistance means giving up all rights. It means expending more time, more strength, and more life, even if this provokes nothing but enmity. For love of one's neighbor — which Jesus equates with love of God — is inseparably bound to unconditional love of one's enemy. The love of God turns to both with equal power. Thus opposition must stimulate love to greater effort; hostility should only strengthen our urge for dedication.

Those who dare to live by this spirit will stand again and again before what is infinite and boundless. They will tremble as before a bottomless abyss, and yet at the same time their lungs will be filled with endless purity and strength, with the eternal breath of God. Their prayer will not be loud and conspicuous, but chaste and hidden. For the Father looks for life in the remote mountain, the barren steppe, and the closed room.

The Sermon on the Mount lies at the heart of John's proclamation: Change yourselves fundamentally, for the kingdom of God is near! Gather no riches for yourselves! Know only one treasure, the treasure in heaven. Do not set your heart on things, for a divided heart leads to darkness and judgment. You cannot serve both God and money.

Worrying about material things is no less godless than accumulating wealth, because God provides abundantly for those who trust in him. He cares for us in the same way that he cares for the birds and flowers and liberates us from both worry and possession. Thus he gives us a simple rule of living: never burden yourself by looking far ahead. Live one day at a time. If you can do this, you will live like children, birds, and flowers, for whom each day is a lifetime. You may break down in guilt and failure, but each day will bring new joy and hope. There will be shadow and nightfall, but sun and air and grace as well.

This is why Jesus tells us to pray and believe again and again. He promises that if we ask, we will receive. The door will be opened to those who knock. The gate is narrow, but it is there for all. And Luke says clearly what the object of this asking, believing, waiting, and daring is. It is the Spirit! And if we who are evil give our children good things, we can rely on God to give us what we need: the Holy Spirit.

Only this Spirit can bring about the material realization of God's new creation. It transforms wolves into lambs and turns the predatory world of humans into the kingdom of God's peace. And its fruits are plainly seen in deeds of love, for action is what marks the new life of the Sermon on the Mount.

—Essay, 1922

•

At the time of Jesus, as today, people were waiting for a new world order. They longed for the kingdom of justice of which the prophets had spoken. Then Jesus came, and he disclosed to them the nature and practical consequences of this justice. He showed them a justice completely different from the moral order of the pious and holy, a living, growing power that conformed to the sacred laws of life. He did not give them commands about conduct, but instead radiated the spirit of the future with his very character.

That character was unity. That is why it is fruitless to take any one command of Jesus out of its context and set it up as a law on its own. It is not possible to take part in God's kingdom without purity of heart, without vigorous work for peace; the change of heart must extend to all areas. It is foolishness to try to follow Christ in only one sphere of life.

The Beatitudes cannot be taken apart. They begin and end with the same promise of possessing the kingdom of heaven. Those who are blessed are characterized by poverty and need, hunger and thirst. And at the same time they possess wealth in love, energy for peace, and victory over all resistance. Their nature is single-heartedness. They are people of inner vision, and they are able to see what is essential. They bear the world's suffering. They know that they are beggars in the face of the Spirit and that they have no righteousness within themselves. But they look to righteousness, and they hunger and thirst for the Spirit.

This is the essence of true religious experience: richness in God and poverty in oneself; becoming one with God and yet always longing for him; firmness of heart and weakness of soul; the justice of God's love and the suffering of injustice.

But wherever there is religious satiety, wherever there is moral self-satisfaction, wherever political achievements or other good works create self-righteousness, where anyone feels rich or victorious, happiness in the fellowship of the kingdom has been lost. Those who believe in God's future keep their hearts fixed on the Spirit and his prophetic justice of love, yet they still feel the injury of injustice in themselves and all around them. They are comforted by the certainty that love shall conquer the earth, but they also know poverty of spirit in themselves and in all humankind.

So they are both poor and rich at the same time. They are people of faith who have nothing in themselves and yet possess everything in God. In spite of failing again and again, they try to reveal God's invisible nature through their deeds. Just as they themselves receive mercy, so they pour out mercy on all in need. They are on the side of poverty and suffering, and are ready to be persecuted for the sake of justice. They know that their opponents' slander will fall on them like hail, yet they rejoice; they overcome opposition with peace and conquer enmity through love.

The people of the Beatitudes are the people of love. They live from God's heart and feel at home in him. The spirit of life has set them free from the law of sin and death; nothing can separate them from the love of God in Jesus. And what is most remarkable and mysterious about them is that they perceive everywhere the seed of God. Where people break down under suffering, where hearts long for the Spirit, they hear his footsteps; where the revolutionary desire for social justice arises, where protest against war and bloodshed rings out, where people are persecuted because of their socialism or pacifism, and where purity of heart and compassion can be found — there they see the approach of God's kingdom and anticipate the bliss to come.

—Essay, 1920–21

AWAY FROM COMPROMISE AND SHADOW

The following essay, written in 1925, is Arnold's response to leaders of the German Youth Movement, who had attacked his efforts for community as "self-delusional, foolish, and mad." Members at the Sannerz community had revoked all rights to private property and held that the way of love, peace, and nonviolence could solve all problems of war and social injustice. They rejected reform as ineffective and held that a new society must be built from the ground up.

Their critics, however, maintained that while it might be possible to avoid holding public office or resorting to law, everyone was tied to the system of oppression and taxation because everyone had to use money, at the very least to buy food. They justified the taking of life "to save perhaps thousands of fellow men" and defended war as "responsible sinning." Further, they argued that body and spirit were in opposition and could never be brought into harmony, that a life of nonviolence in the modern age was "absurd," and that human beings could never "leap over their own shadow." A certain Max Dressler even stated that "the demands of Jesus are not really demands in the actual sense of the word" and that "one cannot speak of discipleship without compromise."

Arnold's answer to these claims is based on the Sermon on the Mount and the First Letter of John.

We must wrestle with the question of compromise because it comes up everywhere and concerns serious-minded people again and again. Behind it the fundamental problem of life lies dormant: the question of evil and death. Evil and death are so oppressive that goodness and life are constantly threatened by them. But it is frightening to see an increasing apathy and compromise with darkness, an avoidance of the either/or of life and death.

There can be no compromise with evil! The word "compromise" has its origin in the language of law. It is a mutual settlement between contending parties, the only solution when legal conflict cannot be resolved.

The question is whether or not one can replace this legal justice with a higher justice: the justice of Jesus' heart as revealed in the Sermon on the Mount. This means that when faced with the threat of a legal battle, we who want the way of life and love must give up everything and allow our opponents to take everything away. If we do this we will be met not by hard demands, but by opportunities for love and joy.

This is the news of the new life: that joy excludes murder; love hates no one; truth strikes no compromise with lying; the heart remains pure only by making no concessions. God makes no settlement with mammon. Joy in life and love for all tolerates no compromise with evil, no concession to loveless indifference or murderous injustice, because love touches all things and changes all relationships. This is the message of the kingdom, the character of Jesus' words. Here is his heart.

Every movement that stems from God points to this way. But whenever Christ's way is forsaken, these movements begin to die. And this process of dying reaches its final stage when there is

no more wrestling with death, when the struggle for life is deserted and people surrender unresisting to the shadow of death —
when materialism and mediocrity gain a foothold and we avoid
the struggle to which Jesus has called us. Such dying threatens
every movement.

Today people try to live simultaneously on the basis of law and
grace. A life of nonviolence is called absurd even though Jesus
lived such a life. People oppose an uncompromising stand, calling it legalism and fanaticism. They affirm materialism without
qualification, are infatuated with sin, and take pains to show that
they can never rid themselves of it. And it seems to make little difference to them whether there is more compromise or less, which
shows all the more how far they are from the Way.

Only the love experienced in the full forgiveness of sin can
bring us healing! In this atmosphere the legalistic "thou shalt"
and "thou shalt not" cease to exist. This cannot be emphasized
strongly enough. Yet the experience of this love must lead to consequences in practical life. Those who are forgiven much love
much. And how can we love God, whom we do not see, if we
do not love the brother or sister whom we do see?

There is only one way: the way of love that comes from
forgiveness and has its essence in forgiveness. This way is the absolute discipleship of Jesus. It makes no compromises with our
cold and loveless age. This does not mean that those gripped by
love never make compromises; rather, the love that has gripped
them can make no compromises. If evil deeds are done, they come
from depravity and weakness of character. But when love takes
hold again, the highest goal reappears and the heart lives again,
full and glowing. The words of Jesus bring back the power of
perfect love.

The First Letter of John describes this uncompromising attitude: whoever claims to be without sin is a liar. We are told this
so that we may not sin. But if we do sin, we have an advocate
who expiates the sin of the whole world. Whoever abides in him
does not sin. If anyone sins, then in this sin that person has not
seen and known him. "We know that we are of God, and the
whole world is in the power of evil."

Those who defend sin show that they have gone astray and lost sight of Jesus. They neither see nor recognize him. There is a great deal of difference between doing evil, and turning our backs on it and forgetting it. For Paul it was essential to leave everything behind and to race single-mindedly toward the goal. Certainly it was always clear to him — and he testified to this strongly — that he was not without guilt. But for him, the forgiveness of Christ meant liberation from wrong and evil. Paul was a fighter in full armor who fought against all evil and even against death itself.

It is significant that uncompromising love has nothing to do with softness or indecision in the face of battle. On the contrary, those who are full of life and gripped by love must be fighters to the point of death. Their battle must be waged most sharply in themselves, against everything that is injurious to life, hostile to fellowship and to God. Yet they can never be hard toward others, though it may be felt as hardness when they struggle with glowing and passionate love against the evil in others and in public affairs. And their fight cannot remain a private matter; it must become a public striving against all evil in all human and social conditions.

Those who work for love in this way will be wrongly seen as moralistic or even legalistic. But their attitude toward people and institutions has been defined by the goal of God's kingdom. Their ethics will be determined by the character of the Son of Man and his followers, by the truth of love, and by the will of God's heart. They must live a life of love in the attitude of the future world and in the perfection of God, because there is no other life.

This brings us to an age-old topic: perfection. Certainly we are not sinless. But today people speak about the necessity of evil and humanity's common bondage in guilt, and this leads to consent to involvement in guilt. Ironically, people dismiss the world peace to which the prophets witness. They reject the elimination of government proclaimed in John's Revelation and the transformation of the present social order through church community. They discount community as the expression of true love.

The fact that they dismiss all these things shows that they no longer take a stand against evil. They are avoiding the decisive choice that Jesus represents: God or mammon. They have turned away from the clarity of Jesus, who challenged us to say yes or no and nothing in between. They have accepted a paradoxical situation in relation to God; all they can say in their vanity is "yes and no" or "no and yes" simultaneously. We must fight against this!

They challenge us: Surely you don't want to wage a general campaign against all evil? And we answer, Yes, this is exactly what it is all about. That is why Jesus came into the world; he called us and sent us out to fight against all evil in all things. He came to destroy the works of the devil. God is light, and in him there is no darkness!

•

Arnold discerned the spirits of good and evil clearly, and though he was compassionate toward those who struggled with sin, he would not compromise when it came to fighting those spirits that opposed life and community. Once, at a retreat center in London, he got into a heated argument with a Swiss theologian. The proprietor, Doris Lester, begged Arnold to calm down. Gandhi had been there the week before, she said, and he had been gentle and quiet, a model guest; couldn't he be the same? But Arnold was not interested in what people thought of him. If he was to call himself a servant of God, he must protest evil, even if by shouting.

GOD'S KINGDOM — FUTURE AND PRESENT

"This is the Sermon on the Mount in the full force of its impact, in its undiminished relevance, in unconditional absoluteness. Here there is no compromise. Whoever wants to belong to the kingdom must give themselves wholly and go through with it to the last!" So writes Erwin Wissman in a 1919 issue of the German periodical Die Furche, *praising a recent lecture by Arnold at a youth conference in Marburg.*

In fact, Arnold cared little for glowing literary reviews, but Wissman is right about "unconditional" and "absolute": this ad-

dress led to the founding of Sannerz, Arnold's community, only a year later. To Arnold, words without deeds were more than foolish; they were dishonest. Scripture was not to be analyzed or interpreted, but to be lived and obeyed. This was hard, even inconceivable, if it depended on human strength or moral will. But it did not; it depended only on new life from the Spirit.

The phrase "future state" is used frequently and underlines Arnold's belief that the kingdom of God is a government, a state in which God rules over human beings.

John the Baptist proclaimed a future state of social justice, God's kingdom, which would come to the earth. He insisted on complete transformation because he believed that God's kingdom was near.

Although crowds of people flocked to him to find forgiveness and renewal, John knew that someone else had to bring the transforming, sanctifying Spirit, without which God's revolution could not take root. This person was the longed-for Messiah, Jesus, whose works followed John's prophetic proclamations. Jesus, too, was directed by the imminence of God's kingdom. Everything he said pointed to the revolutionizing of the earthly life by God.

Jesus baptized in the Spirit. If we allow his words to work in us, we will be stirred by a refreshing wind that penetrates our very bodies. About God's kingdom he said, "What is born of the flesh is flesh, and what is born of the Spirit is spirit." And, "Anyone who is not born of water and the Spirit cannot enter the kingdom of God." Thus he declared that without new birth the future kingdom would be impossible. In this, as in everything else, he lived in the truth that society could be transformed only through a renewal of the spiritual life.

Jesus told us more clearly than any of the prophets what the characteristics of the Spirit are, without which we can gain neither inner renewal nor the future state on earth. In the Sermon on the Mount, he says that the poor, the suffering, the merciful, and the loving are blessed and will inherit the kingdom of heaven. He commands us: Do not lay up treasures on earth for yourself. Turn the other cheek and give away your coat as well as your jacket. Show love to neighbor and enemy alike, help without restraint, and give blessing unconditionally.

How few consider what Jesus really means — what moral demands his words imply! The Sermon on the Mount is known by most Christians, but for many it remains completely closed. Yet in it, Jesus characterizes the inner life that alone can bring about true social justice. It holds the secrets to God's kingdom, and as such can be revealed only in God himself. Only in communion with God we can hope for and take hold of the future kingdom.

It is incredibly dishonest to pray daily that this kingdom should come, that God's will be done on earth as in heaven, and at the same time to deny that Jesus wanted this kingdom to be put into practice on earth now. Whoever asks for the rulership of God must be wholeheartedly resolved to carry out his commands. Those who deem the Sermon on the Mount impractical should remember its concluding words: "Not all who say 'Lord' shall reach the kingdom of heaven, but only those who do the will of my Father in heaven."

God's kingdom is the kingdom of love. This love makes no exceptions, because it is free and cannot be held back. We are surrounded by the relative, the imperfect, the conditional — all that accommodates to circumstance. But those who live like Jesus live in the absolute, the unconditional, and the perfect. They possess God and his kingdom in the present. They are free of the influences of their surroundings. What they are, and what they possess, has a transforming effect on their environment.

Expecting God's future means believing in God's absolute will for the present. The same intensity of inner experience belongs to both; the two are interdependent. And the kingdom of God cannot be of the world as it is today. Yet it is for the world and in the end must transform it completely. Christ's people are sent out to work among humanity, to have an effect in the world, just as Jesus himself did. They must represent the future kingdom, and their task and their actions cannot be different from Christ's: to deliver both soul and body and to heal all suffering and torment.

Like Jesus, they must overcome the temptation to produce

bread by evil means or win control in the realm of politics. All this would be contrary to God's Spirit. They have been sent like defenseless sheep among ravenous wolves and reject all ways of aggression. In obedience to the word of their Lord they have sheathed their swords, for love and the Spirit are their only weapons. They know that this Spirit of Jesus is the mightiest power, which no other power can withstand. He who sent them does not want to destroy life but to save it, and, as children of the spirit, they cannot forget to which spirit they belong. So, too, they cannot send destructive fire on people and cities. The only fire Jesus kindled is the fire of love. There was nothing he wanted more than that this warming light and fire spread over the whole earth.

Jesus knew the resistance in the spiritual realm that had to be overcome before victory could be won. The life of God can be won only by complete firmness of will. The absolute can be won only by totality. This is why the old, degenerate life must be abhorred. One must hate father and mother, wife and child — indeed one's own life, wherever it disturbs and destroys the new life.

This is why Jesus advised the rich young man to sell his possessions, follow him, and live for the poor; and it is why he himself did not have anywhere to sleep. Jesus said to his friends, "Sell what you have. Those who do not renounce all they have cannot be my disciples."

To see this only as a negation of earthly things is to misjudge what is real and essential. Jesus contrasted the richness of gathering treasures to the richness of life in God. Bringing in the richest harvest or erecting the biggest building cannot benefit us if we lose eternal life. Ownership or abundance of earthly goods can never give life. To find true happiness on earth we must be filled with God's love and gather treasure in heaven.

Love, which makes life fully alive, must generate love. It is life's only wealth. The person who overcomes selfishness gains life. Jesus says that the love of God is the greatest love in a person's life, and that we love God whenever we love others as much as we love ourselves.

Jesus had the greatest compassion for the sick and for sinners. Those who have his spirit will be drawn to the victims of prejudice and to those who suffer either through their own guilt or that of others. They will never feel like benefactors, but will know the fulfillment of their deepest calling in service to all people.

He says that such people will remain unconscious of the Christlike character of their lives. They will live for the hungry and the thirsty, the homeless and the naked, the sick and the imprisoned, and yet they will not know what they have done until they are told, "What you have done to the least of these, you have done to me."

Their lives will be so deeply immersed in the spirit of community that none among them will strive for a high position. They will seek the simplest way of serving and help as many as they can. They will love their enemies especially and overcome resistance by genuine affection, by acts of practical service, and by honest intercession.

A life of this nature is possible only if we can become young again and again, if we can become spontaneous and trusting, unconstrained and genuine, loving all people the way children do. Only through childlike trust can we become one with God. "Those who do not receive the kingdom of God like children cannot enter." The kingdom of God belongs to children!

And the kingdom of God rushes in wherever the spirit of childlike love is alive. It is like a man buried alive in an earthquake: at first he flails in the foul, stale darkness, but when he suddenly breaks through the rubble, fresh air rushes in. He is once again united with the world for which he longs, even if he cannot climb out into it. In the same way, we who are imprisoned in the present moment will be overwhelmed by the powers of eternity as soon as we dare to open ourselves to the eternal and absolute, the divine and perfect.

—Essay, 1919–20

•

Those who turn their thoughts away from the physical world and set all of their hopes on life after death are counterfeiters of truth.

The new redemption is intended *for us*. The new will is to be realized here on earth!

Many people over the centuries — most decisively, Jesus — have shown this to be true. But he was murdered, and this was bound to happen. He was killed by the military, by the most organized legal system in history, by the most religious people that ever lived, by the leaders of the church and the voice of the people. And this was no accident. He was murdered because people, bound by their possessions, could not tolerate his witness for truth.

Still today we cannot bear his truth, and so we twist it every way possible. We no longer dare to accept the clarity of his words about loving our enemies, even though everything he taught is contained in his simple words, "What you wish for yourself, do to others."

I am always astonished at those pious people who are concerned for the souls of others and yet have no eye for the need of their starving neighbors. They know quite well what those needs are, and yet they leave them unmet. How can such people confess Christ? We go the way of Jesus only when we leave everything in order to go with him. That means standing up for all people, first of all for the oppressed. This is how he himself lived, and this is how many people have conducted their lives in the course of the centuries.

The nineteenth century distorted the image of Jesus in an amazing way. We are now in a crisis; our actions no longer fit our words. Those who call themselves atheists bear witness to the future of love and to solidarity with the deprived and dispossessed, while those who call themselves Christians are for the most part the possessors and preservers of the status quo. This was not always the case. In earlier centuries not only individuals such as Francis of Assisi but throngs of others hastened to help each other in mutual fellowship.

In this materialistic age we see that the commandment Jesus gave us in his Sermon on the Mount, "Strive first for the kingdom of God and his justice, and everything else shall be yours as well," has not gripped Christendom. Therefore the coming revolution will have to be the overturning and reevaluation of all values, the revolution of all revolutions.

This revolution must be such that it brings with it the brotherhood of humankind. And brotherliness can arise only from the spirit of brotherhood; it will not come unless the starting point and goal and means of fighting are led and determined by the spirit of brotherhood. Therefore I confess to the most decisive and deepest revolution of all: the enormous world catastrophe of all time, the overturning of all things and all relationships, which Jesus called the kingdom of God.

Jesus saw and felt that this coming of the living God to human beings was the only way to true humanity. But this way demands that we enter through the narrow gate. It means the loss of all privilege and property. It means that we perish, that we suffer what amounts in the eyes of others to a personal downfall so severe that it seems we are committing a sort of social suicide. And in a certain sense we are: "Those who love their life will lose it; but those who lose their life for my sake will find it."

We have to lose life in order to find it. This means that our corrupted lives are overcome, that we are freed from the love of possessions, from covetous desire. It is a dying, but it is a dying which allows us to rise to a new life. And this life is not an other-worldly, heavenly life, but a physical life on the earth. It is the life to which the early Christians testified: the life in which our bodies become temples of the Holy Spirit, the life that leads to a community of work and goods.

We are infinitely far away from this goal. But we have to trust in the spirit of life, in the spirit of love and unity, solidarity and justice. In this trust we shall attain not mere equality, but brotherliness and true love.

—Lecture, Hannover, 1923

3

Becoming Human

Nature needs to be redeemed. This does not mean we should be redeemed *from* nature, in the sense of becoming detached from nature, but that nature *itself* must be redeemed, so that matter, the stuff of the first creation, may be freed from the spirit of murder and all other evils. Jesus Christ, the true man, the Son of Man, embodied this redemption in human life.

Unlike those who follow Eastern religions, we who call ourselves Christians need not shed our human nature in order to advance into higher and holier spheres. To the contrary: God became man in Jesus, and this incarnation brings full redemption to us. So we, too, desire nothing else but to become truly human....

— Address, June 1935

THE BETTER RIGHTEOUSNESS

Like his contemporary Herman Hesse, who wrote, "We are not yet men; we are still on our way to humanity," Arnold felt that even twentieth-century human beings — with all their cultural and technological advancement — were not yet truly human. If human beings were not yet perfect, however, Jesus was — and he exhorted his disciples to be as perfect as his Father. In this essay from 1919, Arnold challenges us to the same perfection. He re-

minds us, however, that it must be born of the Spirit and can have
nothing to do with the righteousness of the scribes and Pharisees.

Jesus brings us a new ethic in the Sermon on the Mount. Whereas the morality of the scribes and Pharisees is an outward righteousness — the product of legalism and the coercion of society, church, and state — the new righteousness shows its nature as inner freedom. Independent of outward circumstances, it rejects the impositions of mammon. Instead, it builds upon God and on fellowship with God.

Those who belong to God's kingdom differ so sharply in character from everyone else that they can be compared only to the Father in heaven: "Be perfect, as your heavenly Father is perfect." God is the wellspring of life and love. We become God's children and gain God's character when we are reborn in God's Spirit. But the only way to attain this new life is through liberation from the old.

Jesus himself is the new man, the second Adam, the life-giving spirit who leads us from the deadness of the old nature into the warm, powerful life of the new humanity. In fellowship with him we become the salt which overcomes the decay of death. In him we are the light, spreading life-giving warmth and clarity of vision. In him we gain the nature of God himself, the new nature of spirit and love.

This new life in God is a paradox. We must be decisive and single-minded but at the same time remain humble in the awareness of our utter smallness. God alone can free us from vanity and arrogance, from the piety and moralism of our own strength. Face to face with him we will recognize our neediness and become beggars before him. We will thirst for the righteousness of God.

The righteousness of the moralist is pressured and compulsive, but the righteousness of Jesus is spontaneous. His deeds are driven by enthusiasm for life and by an inner urge for action. And his parable of the good tree with its good fruit — and of the rotten tree with its bad fruit — shows us how to distinguish what is new from what is old. Only those deeds that spring spontaneously from within can be regarded as good. We live the better righteousness only when we bring forth good fruit.

God cannot lie; therefore the new justice is truth that seeks expression in everything. The moralism of the world, the assertion of force and rights, is now replaced by love that stops at nothing — not even in the face of the enemy. This love establishes life and justice. It demonstrates fidelity and purity of thought, and is patient and merciful, full of compassion to the whole suffering world.

God's will is peace and justice. Only those who live by it can claim to be part of his new kingdom. In the same way, Jesus demands deeds and work. We deceive ourselves if we think otherwise. Those who only hear his words are compared to the foolish man whose house, built on sand, collapsed. But those who hear him and act are like the man who builds on rock.

THE CONSCIENCE

There is a modern tendency to call even the healthiest reactions of the conscience a sign of sickness that should be ignored. But that must be repudiated most decisively. The conscience must never be silenced. Instead, it must be led to health by being directed toward the kingdom of God. Far from being despised, it must gain positive recognition through being filled with new clarity and new content. This freeing and fulfillment will lead to lively activity in all areas of life, including areas of public responsibility and vocational activity. In these areas especially, the conscience that is bound to Christ and his kingdom can lead us on completely new ways.

But we live in confusing times, and what was once considered abnormal is now felt to be not only normal but even necessary. The present-day confusion of conscience with regard to sex is typical. In the circles influenced by Sigmund Freud, people attempt to draw all kinds of sexual perversions out of the slumbering subconscious. They actually regret that these perversions have been repressed into the subconscious by the conscience. And what is even worse is the way in which spiritual leaders explain away this ever-increasing confusion, with the result that no one even feels uneasy.

Certainly the word "repression" is enough to deprecate the whole activity of the conscience and throw suspicion on it. In fact, this dangerous word does not apply to a healthy conscience. Yet it is not without significance. There would indeed be a fatal repression, a morbid suppression of all vital impulses, if the conscience were not able to spur the powers of body and soul to positive and creative tasks.

There is a reason why the whole idea of repression is so misunderstood in our sick age: the concept of the family, as it is almost universally accepted today, no longer corresponds to God's creative will. Both young people and their parents lack that sense of inner responsibility that puts the whole of life, including all interpersonal relationships, into God's hands.

Most people today suffer no pangs of conscience when the soul's deepest need for faithfulness is destroyed. They are affected just as little when the smallest souls that want to be called into life are prevented or annihilated. Little souls wait in vain to be called out of eternity. Living human souls wait in vain to be called by constancy and faithfulness. And there seem to be fewer and fewer people in whom the conscience protests clearly and sharply against contempt for the creative spirit, against the profaning of faithfulness and constancy.

The inner protest of the conscience calls us to responsibility and faithfulness in our love-lives. Anyone who calls this "repression" casts suspicion on creation itself. The activity of the conscience provides us with our only safeguard against the fall that threatens us, a fall that would make us lower than the animals. The conscience is not repressed but healthy when we suppress uncreative and life-thwarting urges toward our own body or the body of our companion. We should be thankful whenever "repression" wipes out degenerate or murderous desires.

Enlightened persons do not allow the sultry urges of the subconscious mind to influence the thoughts of their soul. They condemn sinful urges as irresponsible. And they do not regard their sense of responsibility as morbid. Rather, they feel that it is a sign of a healthy mind. A conscience working like this is on its way to recovery; it knows that life's energies are intended for great and noble tasks, tasks that cannot be hindered or desecrated.

As the moral function of the human spirit, the conscience affirms everything prompted and inspired by the Spirit of God. It takes a prophet's place in the human heart: it becomes the mouth of God and must therefore repeat and pass on whatever God has to say. The conscience that is on the way to recovery calls out, "God says it; God wills it; therefore it will come to pass."

The conscience represents the uniting of the human with the divine Spirit in the liveliest way. God's Spirit wants to unite with the human spirit to witness to the truth together. Our conscience will be clear and healthy to the same degree that we have accepted the Spirit of Jesus Christ. Keeping a good conscience depends entirely on keeping the holy faith.

Faith and a good conscience are so closely bound together that rejection of the one means shipwreck to the other. For this reason, baptism of faith testifies to the bond of a good conscience with God. The conscience is made good by faith. Without faith, it goes astray. It becomes a bad conscience. Therefore the apostles of Jesus Christ say about those who do not have faith that they are tainted in mind and conscience alike. This is inevitable because without faith the conscience has no anchor. And the opposite is just as true: if we ignore the compass of the Christ-directed conscience, the ship of faith will be dashed without warning on the next reef.

If we want to fight the good fight to the end, it is just as important to protect our faith as it is to protect our conscience. Faith in the freely given love of Jesus Christ needs to be treasured. A good conscience needs to be protected with the utmost watchfulness. True faith demands a tender and delicate conscience as a fruit of the Spirit. Faith gives birth to a victorious decisiveness against all evil. Faith is served by a sound conscience. Faith demands deeds of love. It is, in fact, love of God, love of Christ, and love of the

Holy Spirit. When we take pains to keep our conscience free of offense at all times, then we are given growth and activity in the grace and knowledge of Jesus Christ, then our inner life becomes anchored in God and in all the powers of God's Spirit. Only love is without offense.

Yet we should not make the mistake of thinking that when our conscience steadily gains health and purity in love, we become sinless! Sinfulness remains characteristic of our nature. But the grace of the sacrificed life of Jesus — the grace of his blood — continually purifies our conscience through the Holy Spirit. Again and again, grace purifies it from all dead works and all offensive actions, from everything that violates the justice and love that go hand in hand with faith. The Spirit of Jesus Christ leads believers to a life that steadily increases in clarity. And yet the believer continues to be bound to all others by a common guilt.

Nevertheless, this guilt has been wiped out. People have the freedom to do good and to avoid evil and to fight it. Step by step, there is an advance toward the kingdom of God. In the life of Jesus, God gave us the gift that takes one burden after another from our conscience. It makes us free, without making us sinless. We do not become gods, but we allow the kingdom of God to come to us.

We can accept God's will in our life only when we are freed from the curse of a bad conscience. We can be one with God's holiness only when our hearts are unburdened, sprinkled, and consecrated. The heart is ready to come before God only after it has been touched by the sacrificed life of Christ in the closest and most intimate way, after it has been met by Christ himself and united with him as he was and is and will be.

Jesus is the way to God. There is no other God than the one who is the God and Father of Jesus. Wherever we seek him, we will find him in Jesus. Unless we are freed in Jesus from all our burdens, we try in vain to draw near to the Father. We have no access to God without forgiveness of sin. And Jesus forgives us by sacrificing his life, by sacrificing his body, his soul, and his blood.

Through Jesus, Satan, the accuser of our brothers, is silenced. The conscience also is no longer allowed to accuse. Even the most murderous accusations that human blood can raise are stilled. If he, the Son of Man, is for us, no one can condemn us. From now on, no accusation can prevent us from approaching God.

The conscience that used to be our enemy becomes in Christ our friend. Before it was in Christ, it had to condemn our life; now it affirms the new life given in Christ. Freed from all impurity through community with Christ, it accepts the assurance and certainty given in Jesus Christ. So the conscience becomes a representative of God. It becomes the voice of the one who is sent by God into the inner land of our soul.

And where the Spirit of God proclaims forgiveness and peace, the conscience will be roused to action. No area of life will escape, for the conscience wages its campaign against all evil. It will advance to the attack so that where there is no peace, peace will be made; where everything is in chains, freedom will dawn. Where injustice rules, justice will take its place; where love has grown cold, joy will break through; where people live for themselves, community will come into being.

—Innerland

•

To fall away from faith, to deny Christ and his love, is the most terrible thing that can happen to us. We are all weak and can fall into sin unless we are protected by the goodness of God. But our love and our confession to Christ should stand unshaken as the deepest thing in our hearts.

Christ is the ultimate voice in our hearts. We can never deny this. If we look into the depths of our hearts, we will find him. We may forget everything else, but not our love to him, our confession to him, our longing for him and our dedication to him. Christ alone can save us. He is perfect, forgiving love. Everything depends on this one thing: do you believe in him? Do you love him?

What good is lamenting our sin? Only one thing matters: that we believe in Christ and that we love and trust him. If we now feel how the whole unhappy world is going to pieces and what an illusion such words as "love," "peace," and "justice" are, then we know there is only one true man, who called himself the Son of Man, the Child of Man. For us, only Christ remains.

I have nothing else to hold on to in life or death; nothing else to believe in for my neighbors, for the people close to my heart; nothing else to trust in for our community; nothing else to hold on to in a world going to pieces. I must confess: I have nothing but Christ alone!

The Holy Spirit is grieved whenever human worthiness — or unworthiness — is put in the forefront. Therefore we ought to look not to human beings, but to Christ. This is especially true for those trapped in a pit, those sunk deeply in the mire. All they can do is wait patiently for the Lord. They must wait until they see the hand stretching down to them, the hand that will pull them to safety and firm ground. That is the right attitude of faith: to wait for God with absolute certainty and with innermost clarity. And such persons, once pulled out of their pit, will not long to return there. No, they will have only one wish: to stay with Christ and share in his love. Christ's love pierces even into the deepest gloom.

That is the Gospel of Jesus Christ. That is why he died on the cross, why he took on the agony of God-forsakenness. And he did this all out of love. That is the Gospel. That is why he arose from the dead: so that he might reign over the living and the dead, so that now we may no longer live for ourselves but for him. This is forgiveness of sin: being sure that his love is greater than all else. However invincible the powers of sin seem to be, however dark the forces of sickness appear, greater than all is the power of love, the forgiving, restoring love that was revealed in Jesus Christ. Therefore let us love him, for he loved us first. Let us believe him, love him, follow him!

— Address, October 1935

4

Unless You Become a Child

Arnold was perhaps unique in the attention he paid to the words of Jesus about children and about becoming childlike. For this reason, he often bemoaned his theological bent, which he saw not only as a gift but also as a curse. He was drawn to children and those people whom others looked down on as simple-minded. And he urged his friends, theologians and philosophers alike, to bow down before God and become children.

Ernst, we are fellow sufferers. We both have a theological vein. This is a gift from God, but it is at the same time a great danger that makes it very hard to live completely from what is genuine, from the depths of one's being, from the direct source of being.

Years ago I wished that I had grown up as an industrial worker. But that was a foolish wish. We cannot change who we are. And yet we must become free from theological introspection; we must be won for the holy cause by a glowing, inner fire. You must become free first from your pronounced tendency to theologize, and second from your own markedly cramped will. Accept your fate: you are a theologian. But now you must become a child!

—Talk, March 1933

•

The kingdom of God belongs to children. For this reason we can be led to the divine truth only if we have the childlike spirit.

Certainly that does not mean that we should not be real men and women; the childlike spirit is not childish but rather unites itself with real manhood and real womanhood. It is the spirit of confident trust, of humility and endurance, the spirit that rejoices and loses itself in the object of its love and is released from self-contemplation. It gives itself completely, unaware of strain and sacrifice, and spends itself as though absorbed in play. It is the spirit of courage, for the true child — like the true man or woman — is never afraid or fearful. It is the answer to all our needs, for the childlike spirit comes from the Holy Spirit. And we must believe that this Spirit really exists and that we can receive it.

—Talk, August 1933

•

Children are open, like open books. They stand in front of us with wide-open eyes; they let us look freely into their little souls. As long as we let them be children, they will tell us right away what they feel: what they like and what they do not like. Genuine children never keep quiet in front of a person's face and then talk about him behind his back. Such cowardly deception is simply not found in children. Children are completely open. They always reveal whatever is in their hearts. And this is how childlike souls act in the church of believers. If they see something that should not be, they speak their mind — directly and at once. They are completely honest and straightforward.

The eighteenth chapter of Matthew's Gospel contains deep words of Jesus about the childlike spirit. To be a disciple should mean to be a learner, to be a child. But the disciples were often unchildlike. They wanted to learn from Jesus, but they were still not of a childlike spirit. They came and asked, "Who is the greatest among us? Who will play the main part? Who will play the first violin? Who will be the greatest in the kingdom of God?" That was when Jesus called a little child before them and said, "Unless you turn around and become like little children, you will never enter into the kingdom of heaven."

If we are like children, we will not think of asking who will be the greatest in the kingdom of God. If we demand to be the greatest and first, we will end up being smaller than the smallest. Those bent on having the right of disposal, on speaking the final word in the church, will not enter the kingdom of God....

Jesus said, "Whosoever receives a child, receives me." When the church receives a tiny child, it receives Jesus, truly Jesus himself. And the word "child" includes all those who have childlike hearts: those who are chaste, who have pure hearts, who do not want to be great, who are unable to show any great accomplishments. Whoever receives such people receives Jesus. Whoever has respect for such a person has respect for Jesus.

The only spirit Jesus acknowledges is the childlike spirit. Thus one of the sternest things Jesus ever said becomes clear: "If any of you corrupt one of these little children, so that he can no longer be a child, it would be better for you to be drowned with a millstone around your neck." Jesus says it would be better for that person not to live: "Woe to the one who is the cause of this corruption! If your hand or foot causes you to sin, chop it off and throw it away. If your eye entices you to evil, pluck it out and throw it away." And he warns us not to hold little children in contempt: "Their angels always have access to my Father."

Remarkable words! How infinitely deep was the insight that set these words, about cutting off the hand or foot and tearing out the eye, next to the words about children. It is better for the church to have the eye that oversees everything torn out, or the hand that guides cut off, than for a child to lose his childlike spirit. It is better to die than to corrupt a child, to take away his childlike spirit.

Anything that puts an end to childhood is corruption. Anything that destroys a child's true nature is corruption. We despise children not only when we mislead them to sin, but when we in any way deprive them of their childlikeness. Therefore Jesus calls us to hold children in highest esteem, to love the childlike spirit, to long for nothing else than to become like children.

—Talk, October 1935

5

Love Divine and Love Human

In this essay from 1921, Arnold maintains that sexual love represents only a small part of the overpowering love of God. As such, Eros is not inherently suspect, but ought to be celebrated — as long as it remains subordinated to Agape. This bold assertion is consistent with Arnold's view that nature itself should be redeemed for God, and that the idea of being redeemed "from" our earthly nature is simply not Christian.

In his *Christmas Carol*, Dickens portrays a rich old merchant in whom all but the last spark of love has died. His life has been ruined because he has given himself over completely to earning money. Nothing but coldness comes from him; he is a man without a heart. This is so tangible that no child or beggar on the street dares ask him for the time of day or approach him for help.

In deathly loneliness he lives a purely commercial existence, devoid of human relationships. He has sacrificed even the love of his youth to the idol of money. Any pure hope he might once have had has been consumed in his quest for recognition and success; every noble feeling has been extinguished in his craving for financial gain. A man of established fortune, he is a soulless being. His life is so completely turned away from the human community that his death is merely the confirmation of a long-established condition. Only if the spirit of his youth once more awakens will his lonely coldness and emptiness give way to God's warmth.

No one can live without love. Those without love are aging and dying; in truth, they are already dead. Where love sickens and degenerates, the innermost life is poisoned. Those who allow love's ardent urge and longing to go unused suffer the loss of their most precious possession.

Deep down, all of us worry about love. All of us feel that love is our destiny. Yet there are many who, in anxious moments, fear the love-life; to these people, love appears as a fire so hot it must be avoided. Others, no more fireproof, come too close to the blazing fire and are burned. They allow themselves to be destroyed in a smoldering fire. Their outward persons deteriorate because they let their inner beings go to ruin.

For most people, love is a labyrinth in which every step seems a blunder. They have not discovered the secret of how to guide the living stream into the right channel. They feel that all love must end in God, just as all rivers flow into the ocean. They realize that much water trickles away or evaporates instead of finding its destination. They want nothing but the fulfillment of their own being and God's being, and yet they lack the vision to separate the pure, original force of love from its weakened forms.

Our language has only one word for the many different degrees of love — including all its sick and deviant forms. This simplicity of expression hides the mystery of love and does not distinguish the relationships of body and soul that are healthy from those that are sick. The Greeks, on the other hand, differentiated between Eros, which includes but is not limited to possessive desire, and Agape, which is divine love, God's all-embracing love that gives itself to all.

People frequently ask how these spheres of love are related. Some are inclined to deny any essential difference between possessive love and personal affection, while others try to separate "holy" love from any contact with Eros. Still others insist that since there can be no radiance of love without erotic energies, divine love does not exist at all.

Only those who have distanced themselves from God can judge in this way. Those who have been overwhelmed by God know that all forms of love, no matter how impure or distorted, are simply reflections of his unending and outpouring love. They are sure that God's holy love alone is what is essential in the love-life and they know that the only important question regarding love is whether it remains in touch with this center of life, or whether it strays from it.

Scientists have pointed out that the areas in the brain responsible for religious experience and for the experience of love are adjacent. Herein lies a deep symbolism that points to the ultimate truth: "God is love; he who abides in love abides in God, and God abides in him." Even the most degenerate and besmirched feelings of love have something from God hidden in them! Sadly, such feelings consume what is of God within them, to the extent that a person drowning in the flesh no longer has any eye for God at all.

Those who squander the energies of their love in the intoxication of the senses deprive the neighboring centers of the brain of their vital power. They exhaust and ruin their feeling for the life of God. They become dull to the noblest impulses that come from the heart of God. Their vision is clouded, and they grope in the dark. But God sees with pure eyes. God floods us with Agape, the divine love that is devoid of lust or possessiveness.

Most people equate Eros with lust, which in its worst form continually exchanges one possession for another. But the erotic life can be ruled by Agape. How often this actually happens is another question.

In this visible world of time and space, we are unable to relate to one another without experiencing the attractions and repulsions of soul and body. This is the sphere of emotionally stimulated love, manifested in the holding of hands, the meeting of eyes, the striding together arm in arm. This is fellowship in word and song, in hiking and sport; it is friendship in joy and sorrow, in faith and in hope; this is the community of humankind without which we could not live.

We rejoice about these powers of Eros that cannot be mistaken for sultry eroticism. For Eros does not represent mere lust, but communal experiences of the soul that belong to a relatively pure atmosphere. Yet the purest air of love is still the breath of the Spirit that goes out from Jesus; Socrates and Plato could only sense this.

The essence and basis of all life and community is Agape, the love that comes from God and leads to God. Agape is the love that never ends and knows no bounds. It is the revelation of the transcendent in the immanent, the revelation of the spiritual in the material, the cosmic in the earthly.

The love between two people or between the members of a community can be fulfilled only in God's inexhaustible and everlasting eternity. Only in God can love flow freely through our lives; only in God can we radiate a love free from the possessive desire of Eros. Only in God can the intoxication of the senses be replaced by the ecstasy of the divine Spirit, which is so often mistaken for asceticism. Eros has submitted to the rulership of Agape. The all-embracing Spirit has replaced the isolated, possessive will.

Nietzsche himself recognized that all love leads to the eternal and the endless: "All desire seeks eternity — deep, profound eternity!" Goethe, too, recognized the power of Eros: Faust at first exults in the physical, but ultimately finds fulfillment in building and preserving the community of humankind.

Our love-life determines our fate in the most serious sense of the word. Either Eros hurls us down into the hellish abyss of demonic self-destruction, or it lifts us up to the pure heights of God. This depends on the inner nature of our love-life, on the nature of the spiritual powers with which we align ourselves. At times we may be unaware whether we have joined with the powers of darkness or with the light of God, but this will become obvious by what effect our love has. One who goes to the harlot becomes flesh and spirit with her. One who enters into the union of two before God and in God experiences rich blessings.

God compares his covenant with his people and the unity of Christ with his church to the union of betrothal and marriage. Christ is the single object of the devotion of his church; he kindles in her all the powers of love and of the Spirit. In the same way, true marriage awakens and unfolds all the powers of manhood and womanhood. This will — to create something beyond the self — should awaken all our energies for the will of God.

But even if the way of marriage is barred by bitter experience or inverted inclination, we can still find happiness through God's love. We must not estrange ourselves from life and love in bitterness, nor stifle the best in ourselves by turning to possessive desires. Rather, we must accept that higher calling in which all powers of love are kindled and revived by the generous, sunny love of God. Then none of love's energy will be wasted or left unused, no power of life suppressed. But we must rise up out of the smoke and fog so that our vision becomes free and our hearts wide; we must open our lungs to the pure air. Here, love comes into its own, love that wants nothing for itself but is fulfilled in lavish giving.

It is true that there is a certain asceticism in the life-affirming love of God, an asceticism that rejects possessive desire. But those who are liberated from the sexual in this way belong to the happiest of people. They are able to love more abundantly than others because their entire time and strength are free, because Agape, God's love, dominates their relationships to others.

Many people who struggle against degeneration and defilement end up embracing a purely negative asceticism. But Jesus did not want this. He had no distrust of life; he joyfully affirmed all those forces of life that are illumined, penetrated, and ruled by God's love. He held marriage and its inviolability in high esteem and honored it by discerning its desecration in the impure thought and the covetous look. He established brotherly love as the sign of his church, and in his own life he embraced all people without anxiety or compromise. He loved the rich young man and yet challenged him to give away all that he had, and he welcomed those who sought redemption from their sick sensuality when he allowed women of ill repute to kiss his feet and anoint his hair. Even on the cross, he gave his mother a son, and his friend a mother.

Jesus transcended the Eros-life completely. He did not stifle emotional relationships, but rather revealed the love of God free from fleshly desire. And God's love is eternal and imperishable. Greed and vanity, possession and property perish before it, as do the highest gifts of language, knowledge, and prophecy. "He who lives in love lives in God, and God in him." Love begets love. He loved first who himself is love; only through him are we able to love.

The warmth that comes from God's heart cannot be produced in any laboratory, by any decree, or by any organization. No friendly effort or zealous benevolence can imitate it. Whoever has felt its unique life-power radiating from the aged or from the wheelchair of a crippled person knows that it is independent of the physical freshness of youth. It is life itself. It is a primary force, an original power of the deepest source.

This Agape knows no bounds of space and time. It is the strength of unconquerable perseverance. It is steadfast faithfulness, and it is equal to every task. It clothes the energy of our love in inexpressible purity, and never injures the modesty or sensitivity of the soul. It is free from inflated arrogance, from pretense, and from presumption for its own advantage. It is real and genuine and has nothing to do with passing effervescence or superficial enthusiasm.

Agape seeks and demands nothing for itself because it lives completely in the object of its love. It knows nothing of rights, and instead finds happiness in giving. It is never harsh, never excited, never provoked to bitterness. It sees both the essential and the potential in everything and does not take into account what might still be evil. Yet it has nothing to do with injustice. It sees through everything that still delays the holy calling of a soul. It wards off all that threatens to obstruct a person's destiny. And it can do this because it is one with God, because it hopes and believes in the final fulfillment of humanity.

No founder of a religion, no philosopher or moralist has lived this love as Jesus did — Jesus, who entered the life of the physical and the emotional. And the love of Jesus is forever and is boundless, or it is nothing. It gives and forgives everything and includes enemies as well as friends. It is not limited by possession or property. It is unconditional and absolute and is never frustrated by outward circumstances. By it, his followers will be known to the world. In it, we no longer look to be loved but seek to love others.

RESPONSIBILITY, DESIRE, AND LOVE

Euripides said that love is the most wonderful thing, but also the bitterest. The gravity of this truth must touch us deeply, for lack of responsibility in love is sin. And the wounding of soul and spirit by irresponsible passion is more murderous than the killing of the body.

Purity is reverence for the meaning of love. The unveiling of the body's secrets and of the mysteries of procreation and birth before many people is a lack of reverence, a betrayal of what is sacred and will remain sacred only if kept for the one great experience of two. A temple is desecrated when it becomes a public place exposed to every profane look.

Reverence for the emotional and physical aspects of love is necessary because the experience of love spans starkly opposing poles. The love-life reaches from the lowest degradation to the rarest heights, from the filthiest breath of plague to the purest air of the spirit. We owe to love the finest productions of art in poetry and music and painting, as well as the entire cycle of nature and life; we recognize in love the basis of civilization and the family. And at the same time we see in love — or what is called love — a consuming flame that drives countless unhappy people into ruin and crime. Love is either abundance of life, of generation, birth, and creation; or else what is called love is sin and death, the poisoning and killing of life.

Moralism has nothing to say to these questions. Civil codes and social traditions cannot be authoritative in regard to the basic forces of life. One need only think of the bondage and slavery of marriage under the German Civil Code, against which the women's movement rightly fought. They wanted marriages founded on faithfulness, not based on the duty of civil law. But what is at stake is not the different forms of church or civil marriage. What we must find is a morality that is altogether higher and deeper.

Sensuality throws itself into ever new channels of untruthfulness and perverse aberration when suppressed by moral compulsion, convention, or legal control. The monastic ideal is no better than the libertine ideal: sexual repression, like sexual subjection, begets oppression and falsity in all other areas of life. To be cold and without desire can never be considered a virtue.

We cannot deny that legalistic morality and neoplatonic introspection have influenced institutional Christianity. But intellectual consideration or social tradition can never be decisive in this fight between life and death. It is not true that "whoever has never exchanged forbidden kisses, never been intoxicated with sinful love...has forgotten how to live!" That which is called sin by the creator of life is always one thing: sacrilege against the soul.

Eros can have no exceptional position in life. The sexual life, like everything else, is subject to the laws of soul and spirit. Thus weakness in this area throws a harshly illuminating light on the lives of people who otherwise seem to show courage and strength of conscience. Impurity never pollutes us from without, nor can it ever be wiped away at will. It breaks out of our innermost depths like an infected sore, poisoning the whole bloodstream, and leaves behind indelible traces on the character and soul.

We are more than body and soul, more than animal. We are spirit. And intellect and reason are not the whole of our being. What is deepest in us is our consciousness of God, God's feeling for the universe, his expectation of future unity in all things. What distinguishes us from animals is our longing for unity of body and spirit, our sensing of the Spirit as the great eternal connection of all living things in love. Even the "atheist" Voltaire confessed that in a land of atheists, love would lead to the worship of God.

Thus Kant was wrong in recognizing only cold duty and sensual inclination. The living soul strives for what is ultimate, for the divine love that is free of lust and self-seeking, for the communal spirit, the outpouring will to love, which stands as much opposed to the covetous sensual will as to moralistic law and order. Our love life will be healthy and happy only when it is guided by this ultimate will.

Our love for each other must be redeemed. With Augustine, we must pray that its "ardent fervor for the world become an ardent fervor for the Master of this world":

Love, but take care what it is you love. Love is the self of the soul, the hand of the soul. When it holds one thing, it cannot hold something else. If it is to hold what one gives it, it has to put down what it is holding. The one kind of love is turned toward community, the other is limited to the ego; the one looks to the good of all and thinks of the spiritual fellowship, the other tries to bring even the cause of fellowship under itself. The worth of persons is not to be assessed according to what they know, but according to what they love.

— Essay, 1928

THE NEW MORALITY

Until Jesus appeared, the greatest goodness anyone could offer God was moral endeavor. People strove strenuously toward an ideal, scrupulously obeying commands and prohibitions, repressing and stifling contrary inclinations, and frantically attempting to deny and mortify the flesh. They tried with human strength to ascend the mountain where the light would not be obscured nor the air polluted. But Jesus brought a justice better than anything human effort could achieve and different in every sense from what the law and the prophets offered.

Even so, the law and the prophets reveal God's being and will. Jesus did not undo or obscure in any way the clarity of their revelation; those who try to break down these moral commandments are desecrating that which God has laid in the conscience. In doing so, they lose their security against the powers of lying, hatred, and greed, which then hound them from one situation to another until they finally fall prey to death.

Not one letter of these ethical commands and moral prohibitions can be canceled until the essential spirit of these laws has been revealed and has taken on flesh and life. These commands express the holy "thou shalt" of our inner calling, the holy "must" of our inner destiny — the only absolute that lives in the human soul. More and more people reject one after the other of these laws today, declaring them null and void. They will be poorly prepared for God's kingdom.

Before the word became flesh in Jesus, God expressed the essence of his holiness in a form at once demanding and forbidding. His will had to be expressed in the letter of the law, because there was no living heart to give it expression. The law must still take over where greed rules and where the truthfulness and purity of Jesus has not yet taken root. The state with its coercive power and the law with its statutes are a necessary safety valve for the chaotic mass of humanity which, like steam in a boiler, would explode if unrestrained by the iron vessel of governmental force and the safety valves of its laws.

But as soon as people are gripped by God's love, all of life is different. They grow close to one another and become organs of a mystical body, ruled by the spirit of unity, one heart and one soul. The necessity of force and coercion, of law and moral striving, is removed; the true spirit, which the law expressed imperfectly, comes to rule. The new righteousness of Jesus, the goodness of heart and divine strength that embrace all human existence, is not bound by restraints of legal relationships.

The scribes and Pharisees had a firm conviction, a moral direction, and an iron will. They were better than their reputation; they were morally upright, devout figures who commanded respect — individuals who felt deeply their responsibility for their people. But they lacked the free spirit that blows from God: the gift of life that grows and bears fruit.

The new justice is God's goodness. God's nature cannot be imitated or created, and nothing can replace God's power. So too, the works of the first love cannot be artificially manufactured. No intelligent reflection, no resolution or effort, can produce the warmth of heart that is God. Where God is alive, active love takes the place of dead moralism.

— Essay, 1920

6

Love Is Work

Working together with others is the best way to test our faith, to find out whether or not we are ready to live a life of Christian fellowship. Work is the crucial test of faith because such a life can come into being only where people *work* for love. Love demands action, and the only really valid action is work. Christian fellowship means fellowship in work.

—Talk, May 1934

•

Though he could never escape his privileged upbringing or scholarly bent, Arnold loved the working class. He abhorred the sterility and mechanization of factory work, but rejected the notion that all physical work was demeaning; he asserted that farm or garden work was not only healthy but necessary for the development of the soul. Thus he found joy and relaxation in turning compost and gardening and did not hesitate to hand a second pitchfork to the many visitors — including young idealists and intellectuals — who came to him hoping for theological discussion. Irmgard Keiderling, his secretary, remembers seeing him at the manure pile with the mayor of Quedlinburg, a town councilor from Munich, and even the local doctor from Hanau.

Justice and love demand that everyone take part in simple practical work with a spade, hatchet, or rake. Everyone should be ready to spend a few hours each day in either the garden or on the field: digging and spreading manure, plowing, or hoeing potatoes; on the reaper, at the circular saw, or in the locksmith's shop. Everyone should be ready to devote a few hours every day to this practical work; those who have done purely mental work till now will feel its humanizing effect especially.

In this way it will be possible for each person's unique gifts to be kindled. The light that flickers within each heart will then exhibit its once-hidden glow in scholarly research or in music, in expressive words, in wood, or in stone.

—Essay, 1920

•

In his enslavement to the principles of investment and profit, the much-admired industrial magnate Henry Ford has achieved the very utmost in soul-killing enslavement to dead machinery. He has robbed work of its soul to such an extent that 79 percent of all the operations in his industrial plants are performed by completely unskilled labor. Forty-three percent of his workers require only a day's training; another 36 percent require only eight days. Only 21 percent of all the workers, mechanics, and foremen he employs are allowed to put even a little thought and skill into his famous cars. The great majority — the other 79 percent — are imprisoned in their work as soulless slaves. They are condemned to a humdrum existence, sacrificed to capitalist profit.

—Lecture, March 1925

COMMUNITY AS WORK

In this address from 1921, Arnold speaks of the church as a living organism: a dynamic, changing, growing, and living body that reflects the communal order of the natural world. His metaphors reflect a thorough knowledge of modern biology, and he draws heavily on this knowledge to emphasize the necessity of community not only for plants and animals, but for women and men as well.

Community presupposes life. We know that life is community
of life, and that there is no life that is not living community. We
can see this clearly from the community the hermit crab enjoys
with the sea urchin in the depths of the sea. These remarkable
crabs have soft and sensitive backs, and so defend themselves by
crawling into the shell of a dead snail. But even there they are
not yet safe from the polyps, those extraordinarily dangerous and
ravenous creatures of the deep sea, which can pull them out of
their shells with their tentacles. So the hermit crab forms a settlement community with the urchin, which fastens itself to the
snail shell in which the crab lives. This urchin, with its prickly
arms, clutches the whole shell so firmly that it seems almost impossible to loosen it. Thus the urchin protects the hermit crab
from danger.

The crab also contributes to this mutual relationship. It provides mobility for the otherwise stationary urchin, allowing it
to catch any prey that might cross the path of the wandering crab. Each creature shares its surplus with the other. These
two creatures arise from such irreconcilably different genera that
no sexual relationship could ever exist between them. Yet from
time immemorial, they have represented a relationship of life as
community and community as work.

But we do not need to descend into the depths of the sea to
see other examples of the same kind of thing. In the mountains,
for example, we can find the lichens: fungi that live in community with algae. These two very different plants are unable to live
without each other. Only in community are they capable of life.

On a different level, colonies of ants or bees live in a primitive
and yet powerful common life, sacrificing themselves as workers
to provide for the propagation of the greater colony by the queen.
These insects show us humans something which, in our desire
for progress, we have lost with miserable weakness: the social
instinct for the context of life, and for the common challenge.

There are many other examples from the practical life of the
animal world. But we do not need to look for extraordinary and
interesting examples in the world of nature alone. There is also a
church-community of men and women on this earth! Humanity

is of course divided; we have not yet arrived at earth-wide community. But the fact that this church-community exists is reality. And if we want to understand life-community, the mystery of this emerging, growing church-community must dawn on us.

This church has nothing to do with any denomination or sect. The mark of the emerging church and the coming kingdom is the building up of quiet, hidden life-relationships, beginning with tiny cells which constantly renew their relationships with each other, become organs and members, and then again become one in a single body.

This church cannot be brought about by authoritative decisions, laws, or regulations. No human effort can bring it into existence. No dictatorship can prepare for it or create it. It is far from anything our self-will can achieve — far from all the efforts of self-seeking, power-hungry persons or groups. It can come only as a gift of the Creator's spirit of love.

But for this very reason, we must guard against the false notion that God is a purely transcendental power, removed from matter and the stuff of this earth. The coming community of life will be a kingdom of work on this earth. Work will be the binding factor in the cells of human community. The only work we can do with our whole soul, work full of spirit and pulsing life, comes from love. And there is no love that does not get to work.

Love is work: practical, strenuous work of muscle and mind, heart and soul. The kingdom of love, therefore, must be a kingdom of work. Work, truly unselfish work, animated by the spirit of brotherliness, will be the mark of the future, the character of the humankind to be. Work as spirit, work as living reality, such as we all have lost, work as dedication in enthusiastic love of togetherness — that is the fundamental character of the future. Joy in togetherness will show as joy in work.

How infinitely remote present-day humankind is from work like this! And since today we have only a faint conception of the possibility of this common life, we will be troubled again and again by pessimism, like a shadow from the abyss.

But we do know that it is not some fantastic, unattainable future; on the contrary, it is the quiet reality of a church already emerging today. God is — everywhere and always. We cannot make the kingdom of God — that is impossible — but we can live in God's kingdom all the time. Christ comes to us. And as certainly as this is true for individuals, it will be fulfilled as fact for the whole world.

We are on a rope stretched tautly between two worlds. Let us walk out on this rope toward the land for which we long! If we believe this kingdom is approaching, if we are sure of this final transformation of all things, then let us live now in accordance with the spirit of this future.

Just this is the mystery of the emerging church, germinating and blossoming among us in secret: that we can live and work already now, here and everywhere, in the community of the Spirit. Faith in God and faith in Christ is the power that makes this possible. Where alienation and hostility prevailed, people will find the relationship to one another which is community.

JESUS AND THE FUTURE STATE

Jesus repeatedly challenges us to work while it is still day. He compares his kingdom to labor in a vineyard, to the careful investment of entrusted money, to the good use of one's talents. If God's kingdom is to transform our vale of tears into a realm of joy, then God's kingdom must be a kingdom of work. Work alone befits the destiny of the human spirit.

Our very nature calls us to a life of productive labor. We will find joy in life only by joining in the untainted fellowship of work. Those ruled by the spirit of mammon hold that human beings take no pleasure in work without profit. But that is a lie; in reality, what makes us truly happy is our deep vocation to work: our urge to get a job done, to do something worthwhile, to give practical help. True happiness is found not in making money, but in the productive and successful use of our strength — though we must each find that activity which suits us best, which corresponds to our particular gifts, interests, and inclinations.

It is commonly argued that this is utopia, that no one would perform menial tasks unless compelled. But such reasoning arises only out of the debased morality of our modern-day humanity. Most people today are unable to find any joy in simple or lowly tasks. Yet at the same time, they affirm quickly that the difference between so-called respectable and degrading work disappears when they are caring for a loved one. Love ignores these distinctions; whatever we do for the beloved person seems good to us.

That so many people value the work of the mind over physical labor shows the unhealthy state of our society. Human beings are simply not meant to concern themselves continually or exclusively with lofty ideals and spiritual matters. Those who seek only intellectual sophistication will one day pay a bitter penalty: a rude awakening to life's ugly realities. True, our intellectual life needs to be stimulated and deepened if we are to become human. But only when we know the pleasures of physical labor will we experience the joy of being — joy in God and joy in God's creation.

A person who feels estranged from nature is sick. Healthy people long to exercise their bodies, to do simple farm work, to be in the sun and the light, to make friends with woods and mountains, to touch plants and animals, to feel the soil. These longings may have receded before the pressures of our big cities with their hypercivilization, but in the end they will break through all the more forcefully.

Tolstoy's Russian peasants may thus surprise us with their primitive bliss, which seems to depend on the possession of a sound body and the ability to work with healthy hands. But this spirit of loving dedication bestows on their experience of nature a profound consciousness of fellowship, through which the simplest physical activity becomes a source of bounteous joy. Such joy cannot even be imagined by the depraved hedonists of our sham civilization.

People will never stop longing for a life of simple fellowship in nature. To take pleasure in nature, to work with nature — as well as to deepen the intellectual life and to be creative in works of love — these things are the immediate objects of our longing. It is not in keeping with God's will that these ends should be opposed or disparaged. In fact, we cannot even attain these things on our own. They can be given to us only by God.

•

The love of Jesus bought and won us before we were born, when we were still his enemies. This love is like the sun calling the greenness of life out from the deadness of winter. The sun, God's love, awakes us from death to life. It comes to us in Christ, and it brings forth the fruit of deeds: activity and labor.

The unfruitful tree is under a curse. Woe to the church where Jesus searches in vain for deeds, for action and work in keeping with the life he has awakened. For he died just for this very reason: that we not live for ourselves any longer, but that all who have life live for him who died and rose for their sake. That means surrender. It means overcoming the selfish life, overcoming all self-interest and private property. And for this to happen we must be moved and urged by the love of God.

There is a legend about a proud hunter who was snatched from the threat of imminent death by the timely intervention of a passing traveler. From that moment on, this hunter lived for nothing other than the daily service of his rescuer. He undertook no other work or occupation but this. He remained constantly in attendance upon his rescuer. So it must be with us, if we want to live for Christ. It is not enough for followers of Christ to devote to Jesus only those few hours which their middle-class profession or business leaves free. Just as Jesus dedicated his whole life to us, so we too must leave our vocations and our businesses in order to live for Christ and his church.

All of us are invited to the banquet of his kingdom. The table is set; everything is prepared. But if we are unwilling to come because of our fields, or because of our oxen or the management of our farm or business, or because of our marriage, or any other personal concern — then we are under the wrath of God and have no part in community with God. Those who surrender their strength to the service of the church must leave forever their own occupations and interests. Perfect love to Jesus means devoted communal work. And we can achieve this love only when we receive the perfect love of his surrendered life—his death and his resurrection.

The most terrible reproach that Jesus can direct against a church is when he says, "I have this against you, that you have left your first love." No one should be resigned to such a depressing development. As long as we bear even the faintest spark of love of Jesus within us, we cannot remain unmoved. His call must pierce our hearts: "Think, think, from where you have fallen."

There is no other conversion to the first love but that of deed. Therefore Jesus goes on: "Repent, and do the first works of love." If we do not get as far as deeds and works, then we are not converted. For if our love to Jesus is sincere, it will compel us to surrender all our bodily strength and mental and spiritual energies. Service in the church is the only deed that can possibly be meant by the first work of the first love. If love has truly taken possession of us, we will do our utmost in the daily life of the church.

None of us can claim a personal savior just for ourselves; it is the mystery of faith that all members of the church believe in the same Christ. The church is one body; there is one Spirit and one hope; there is one Lord, one faith, one baptism, one God, and one Father. And in this unity the love of Christ, in its breadth, length, depth, and height, surpasses and exceeds all understanding.

7

From Isolation to Community

Religion and devout feelings are useless unless they are expressed in action and in truth, that is, in real community. Jesus says, Love God! And his other command is exactly the same: Love your neighbor! We cannot love God if we do not love our neighbor.

— Public address, September 1935

CONSCIOUSNESS AND COMMUNITY

"No man is an island, entire of himself." If this is true, it follows that we are communal beings — and that the basic sickness of people today is isolation and egocentrism. The remedy Arnold prescribes is a greater consciousness — an awareness of the people around us and ultimately an awareness of God — that leads inevitably to community.

I

Each human being is a coherent organism. All the organs in the body, and the individual cells within them, invigorate and serve each other, giving and receiving life through the same bloodstream. This is the secret of the living body: its many diverse members and activities are integrated into one whole. Each part of every organ contributes to the structure of this whole. And even the individual cells that make up these parts draw life from ever smaller units.

Life consists in overcoming isolation through community. This is true even in the most primitive cells we can observe in nature. No primitive cell lives for itself. Its life depends on reciprocal relationships with other cells. Its very division is a sign that it does not want to live alone, that it cannot live in isolation. It would rather divide itself into two living creatures than go on living in isolation.

At all times and in all places, individual organisms build creative, living relationships in order to serve one another. Life is community. There is no other life!

We may well be tempted to ask whether our stomachs and ears, for example, are truly conscious of the unity of the body, or whether they are not separate beings assembled within the body simply for their own limited ends. But to grasp all this is impossible. All we know is that no matter how individually complex our various organs are, the body functions only when they are linked by a single pervading consciousness into a unified organism.

II

Babies begin to sense their own unity of consciousness very early on, though of course differently from us adults. They feel that not only the parts of their own person but also everything they see, everything that happens to them, belongs to their consciousness as a whole. Babies do not regard their bodies as the boundary of their existence. They see farther than we do. The toy hanging over their carriage appears to them just as much a part of their lives as the fingers they move or the toes they put into their mouth. Subconsciously, they live with a unified awareness of all they perceive through their senses and experience. There is unity about everything that enters their consciousness.

Later they begin to draw distinctions. They begin to speak of themselves in the third person: "he" wants the bottle, or "she" wants some other thing. Later still, their growing realization of themselves as individuals emerges; they now speak of themselves as "I" and strongly emphasize the demands of this "I." In this period of healthy egoism, they assert the "I" of self over the greater "we" of community. But once they recognize — however slowly and reluctantly — the limitations of the individual self, they look again for community with people and animals. And more — the true child senses a mystery above and beyond these: the great "Thou" of God with his stars, angels, and spirits.

We adults lose this feeling for community quickly. Very easily, we reach the point at which we feel ourselves to be quite separate: entirely independent units of consciousness that are perplexed by the very existence of other conscious units. And in our egocentric state, we are amazed that other people make the same sort of exaggerated claims to self-importance as we do. We are completely taken up with our own small selves, both in our secret thoughts and, above all, in our basic attitude to life.

The nineteenth-century German philosopher Max Stirner has written about this problem quite frankly:

> What is the purpose of my dealings with the world? I want only to enjoy the world; therefore it must be mine. Thus I need power over the world. I need to make it my property; that is, I need to take advantage of the world and the people in it. My happiness comes at the cost of their happiness, but I will never sacrifice myself. I am an egotist and I relish it! And I am not one ego among others; I am the only ego. I am unique.

None of us should imagine that we are far removed from this extreme egotism. We need to ask ourselves honestly if we do not, at least in our private lives, live exactly as Stirner describes:

> I exist only for myself. Everything I do, I do to expand and protect my sphere of influence. I am "good" to people only to take pleasure in them and to assert myself and increase my power. And I wrong all those who might hinder, disturb,

or restrain me, who stand in the way of my enjoying life. I live for myself and for nothing else.

The history of philosophy, especially in the West, shows us where such thinking leads. Philosophic egotists, believing themselves to be the only source of all their thoughts, cannot help but tell themselves: "I certainly see people talking, and I see others listening and acting, but this all has no objective existence. It exists only in my mind. I believe in only one thing — my own existence."

There have been thinkers, for example, who have laid an empty book on the table and asked themselves what they could write in this book that was perfectly certain. One of these philosophers concluded: "I think, therefore I am. I am, since I have a consciousness."

And it is surely the most remarkable step in this whole progression that still more radical doubters have had to cross out this proposition as well. They have lost even the certainty that they themselves exist. This last doubt puts into question the one thing that the isolated individual thinks about — one's own small ego — and should lead beyond the limits of knowledge: to belief in God.

Most people, however, hold on to the assurance that because they think, they are.

III

Consciousness itself demands that we recognize this state as a mortally diseased condition. But healing can begin immediately when we recognize our origin in that source where there is not isolation but vibrant unity. Just as children's awareness reaches beyond the bounds of their own small bodies, so the consciousness of healthy persons reaches out far beyond their own minds. True consciousness is all-embracing. Its cosmic outlook goes beyond the bounds of the whole world. Ultimately, it is consciousness of the divine.

Consciousness wants to comprehend everything, to penetrate everything. It is not content with what I am as an individual and what I do within the limits of my individuality. Consciousness pushes me to measure the breadth and depth of the earth, of the entire universe. Consciousness demands the impossible: it wants me to survey the entire history of life, to understand its deepest relationships.

Consciousness demands that mind and spirit strive for what is infinite. It demands totality and universality. It demands the whole, the comprehension and penetration of the whole of life. It is hostile to isolation in every form.

In its longing for infinity, it points to the Source and the Creator — to God. Life and community exist in God alone. God is the Spirit that surrounds and connects all things. He rejoices in the self-sacrificing relationships of everything that lives. And he creates unifying life in the face of isolating death.

IV

Healthy persons see and act in love. They have been redeemed from isolation and are turned to God. Their love goes out to all. They are no longer preoccupied with themselves, but look at themselves in the context of the whole. They know quite well that they are meant to exist, but they are certain that life does not come from themselves; they feel themselves to be part of a greater whole. They know that the Holy Spirit is the only power that makes everything truly alive. So their affirmation of life finds voice in different words than their previous self-delusion did.

Conscious of their smallness and limitation in the face of the greatness of their calling, they can only say, "I am, for I am being thought. I am alive, for I am being lived! I have been created and called by the consciousness that penetrates all things." They place their life under God, under the comprehensive whole.

Persons who are on the way to health have to grasp the whole and live for the whole. They throw their own small, incapable self — which nonetheless has been called — into the great task of the comprehensive consciousness. They permit their own ego to flourish only insofar as it brings fruit and life to the whole.

V

Each of us suffers from separation and isolation. We are sick and dying, diseased to the core. Our very life is death. But before we can attain the health and vitality of true life we must diagnose our illness; we must recognize that we ourselves are the cause of this disease. Our thoughts are repeatedly bound up within ourselves; fundamentally, we are able to see only our own point of view. We constantly call attention to ourselves and fight for our own advantage, for our own small existence.

It is unhealthy for a single organ of the body to force itself on the whole. The loud pumping of the heart during climbing, cycling, or rowing tells us that something is out of order. In the same way, a stab of pain in the chest, or worse still the coughing up of blood, makes us keenly aware of our lungs. We are forced to concern ourselves with them, because it is clear that they are sick.

It is exactly the same with the individual person within the community of humankind. When individuals make themselves noticeable — when they call attention to themselves, emphasizing and giving prominence to their own ego — then it is obvious that they are sick. They are in danger of destroying the contexts necessary for healthy life. This is seen most clearly in people with hysteria and neurasthenia, those whose minds and bodies collapse under the strain of worry and depression. We all know such people; perhaps all of us are even like them to a greater or lesser degree.

We all know the unhealthy state in which we try to impress those around us by making outlandish remarks. If this does not succeed, we attempt to attract attention by witticisms and jokes. When this does not work, we force people to notice us by angering them with our insolence. When even this fails, some induce hysteria, shivering, weeping, fainting, or even attempting suicide. Such extremes succeed in forcing everyone around, however unwilling, to notice them.

The diseased ego turns to audacious and peculiar behavior because it can no longer attract attention through talent or achievement. And it remains sick as long as it lets its own little self come to the fore, as long as it is touchy and hypersensitive, as long as it feels pushed into the background, as long as it seeks preferential treatment. This disease is fatal: it is a sign of inner decomposition. An obtrusive ego exposes a disintegrating life.

The sickness of the world lies in this isolation of the accentuated ego. Individuals who feel no pain but their own cannot identify with the world's suffering. They care only for themselves, fight only for their own existence, and seek only their own improvement and happiness. In this way, they increase the suffering of others. They are parasites that endanger the whole. They have severed themselves from the reality and unity of life. They have cut themselves off from the whole and must finally perish.

The only thing people really have in common today is suffering. This should call us to solidarity. But we cannot speak of solidarity and interdependence without speaking first of joy, joy in others, which is love. This joy should be the common property of all, but it is not. Most working people are cut off from all access to joy — cut off from the practical possibility of a communal life. People do hope for better days, however, and this is important; apart from this faith in the future, there is no reason for them to help each other.

The subconscious behavior of our own bodies demonstrates unity of action for the good of the whole. If a finger is hurt, for example, the whole body becomes involved and is drawn into active sympathy. The injured member conveys its message of distress to the rest of the body, and within minutes a powerful defense force has been assembled; defenders rush to the place of attack from all parts. When one member suffers, all members suffer with it. We see the same courageous interventions in humankind as well, when we meet each other with love and joyful assistance.

It is deadly for one member of the body to withdraw from mutual service. It is demonic when an individual organ breaks away from the rulership of the uniting soul. This separation of body and soul is most obvious in diseased sexuality, but it is present as well wherever the individual will separates itself from the spirit of the whole.

The demonic power of self-centeredness rules personal and public life everywhere. It dominates political, social, and even religious groups to the extent that they emphasize their own exclusive goals and interests, acting autonomously and acknowledging only their own, self-serving laws. Such groups have turned their backs on the spirit of community. They do not give themselves wholly in the service of others, because they are estranged from the spirit that leads to future unity. They evade the creative and renewing power that transforms crumbling matter into coherent life. They lack the impulse of life, the joyful dedication in love to all that is alive.

The need of the world results from this one disease: isolation as world suffering and world suffering as isolation. But the spirit of love can heal us and bring us back to unity, unity in common work and fellowship. And this spirit of love is already alive, amid all division and death, in the hidden, mysterious working of God's living church.

—Essay, 1927

•

Living or working together with other people, even those who supposedly share our ideals and goals, can be extremely difficult. Joy in one another quickly gives way to irritation, and then gossip and finally betrayal, when we allow ourselves to be annoyed by a person's character or way of doing things. The solution, according to Arnold, is forthright honesty and humility.

There is no law but love. Love is joy in others. What, then, is anger at them? Words of love convey the joy we have in the presence of our brothers and sisters. It is out of the question to speak about another person in a spirit of irritation or vexation. There must never be talk, either in open remarks or by insinuation, against any brother or sister, or against their individual characteristics — and under no circumstances behind their back. Gossiping in one's family is no exception. Without this rule of silence there can be no loyalty and thus no community.

Direct address is the only way possible. It is a service we owe anyone whose weaknesses cause a negative reaction in us. An open word spoken directly to another person deepens friendship and will not be resented. Only when two people do not come to an agreement quickly is it necessary to draw in a third person whom both of them trust. In this way they can be led to a solution that unites them on the highest and deepest levels.

—August 1925

•

Touchiness, opinionatedness, self-love, and self-centeredness: all these are obstacles to the common life. To have a higher opinion of oneself than of others is a deadly poison; it renders a person completely incapable of living in community. Such persons can never experience what is crucial: the unity of the great cause. They suffer from a disease that will destroy body, soul, and spirit.

People who live with themselves in the center — who think about themselves all day long, who see everything in relation to themselves and from their own point of view — are seriously ill. They are mentally disturbed. They are far from becoming true brothers and sisters. They are lost even in the midst of a communal household.

We are inclined to see the shortcomings of others far out of proportion to our own weaknesses. If we look carefully, however, we will see that we are actually all the same. We must become reconciled to human imperfection. And self-centeredness is a lying spirit. It is completely false. Those who have such a high opinion of themselves that they cannot admit to making mistakes are living in the deepest untruthfulness and insincerity. Their egotism must be condemned, not only because it does not fit into community or because it is morally wrong, but also because it brings death and destruction.

Self-centered people are mortally sick. They must be redeemed.

They must recognize that Christianity has an objective content, that it is a cause for which we can completely forget ourselves and our own little egos. Self-importance is nothing but autosuggestion. It leads to hypocrisy. And unless we are freed from all posturing, from all affected holiness, we are utterly lost.

The people who are most endangered are those who see God from their own point of view and make God relate to themselves. But God's cause is a cause for which we are not needed. We are not indispensable. We are not just unimportant; we are an obstacle. We are adversaries of the cause. Redemption cannot begin until we recognize this and see ourselves, and our piety, as adversaries. Until that happens we are deluding ourselves.

We are not the truth, and because we are not the truth we cannot and should not place our own persons in the center of our thoughts. We would make idols of ourselves. The cause must be in the center. And redemption from the life of self, from wanting to be in the right, from imposing our own ways, comes only through a cause that exists completely outside of our own selves.

We human beings can recognize light only in contrast to shadow and darkness. We can grasp the cause only through an awareness of its adversaries, for we are not gods but human beings. Think of a campfire: when it is lit at night, we who sit around it are illuminated even though we remain seated in the dark. But it is the dark background that makes our shining faces visible.

Those who are still in love with themselves cannot recognize the cause; nor can they who are still in love with their own religious experience, their conversion and rebirth. Not until we see the great cause against the wretchedness of our own insignificant beings will we grasp its greatness.

In the early church the Holy Spirit came to people only after they had recognized themselves as the murderers of the long-awaited Messiah, as adversaries of the Holy Cause for which they had always striven. We are afraid of this awful awakening, especially if we have sought for years or decades to live holy lives and suddenly recognize ourselves to be murderers and adversaries. That is hard but necessary.

Paul was blinded when the Spirit came upon him, and it was not exaggeration but deep conviction that led him to say, "I am the worst of all men." He had been personally responsible for the persecution of the church, for the murder of Christian martyrs. Paul had to recognize that he was a persecutor of the Messiah, a persecutor of the kingdom of God. Not until he recognized this could he become an apostle of God's cause. This cause, which Karl Barth rightly says is "totally other" than what we ourselves are, is the only thing that can free us from our self-centeredness and touchiness, from our opinionatedness and our quarrelsomeness, from all that makes us unfit to live in community.

But unless we recognize ourselves as adversaries we will never grasp the greatness of the cause. People who make vows on the basis of their own radicalism, their own piety, or their extreme "thoroughness" are incapable of standing firm. Their vows are bound to collapse in disgrace. But a vow that springs from the cause and for the cause, a promise that leads us away from self, simply cannot be broken....

—Talk, August 1933

•

Even when Arnold's own children were still quite young, he took in both homeless tramps and unwanted pregnant women. He saw Christ in everyone he met, and welcomed with love each one who came to his door. Karl Keiderling, who came to Sannerz in the 1920s, arrived with dirty clothes and wild, unkempt hair. Though a complete stranger, he was embraced as an old friend: "We've been waiting for you," Arnold said, and he meant it.

Love sees the good Spirit at work within each person and delights in it. Even if we have just been annoyed with someone, we will feel new joy in them as soon as love rules in us again. We will overcome our personal disagreements and joyfully acknowledge the working of the good Spirit in each other.

Augustine goes even further. He says we ought not to see each other as we are now, but that we should see others as they are meant to be, as they will be when God's Spirit fills them completely.

—Talk, March 1933

FROM PRIVATE PROPERTY TO COMMUNITY

For Arnold, community was the answer to all of life's problems. And he believed in community not because of any one biblical commandment, but because he felt that the very life of Jesus — and the witness of the entire New Testament — pointed toward it. But he did not stop at mere intellectual or even spiritual recognition of this truth; rather, he pursued it to the point of practical realization. The result was community: community of goods and community of spirit.

Humanity writhes in agony, on the verge of death, and the most obvious sign of its mortal sickness is private property. The root of property is separation and disintegration, decay and corruption. These ills arise through self-isolation, through the self-seeking of the covetous will. Private property destroys the relationships we have with each other and with God.

Private property is the root of murder, the cause of war, the cause of vicious competition in business. It leads to prostitution and marrying for money, which are really the same thing, and is the cause of dishonesty in business and of every other kind of lie. Our entire economy is based on greed, on the profit motive, on people's urge to self-preservation and their craving for greater power.

Jesus rightly said that if the kingdom of Satan were divided against itself, it would have fallen long ago. But our highly developed capitalist economy does not fall, because the demonic forces of greed work hand in glove with each other. They all follow the same line. The possessors thus become possessed.

When one sphere of human activity sets up its own laws, irrespective of all others, it becomes an idol. Then we are ruled by demons; life is rent apart and torn into shreds. This worship of idols — the worship of money and property — is the curse of our century.

People defend their collective egotism by explaining that they don't want their property for themselves, but for their wives and children. They say they don't fight wars to protect their own personal property, but to protect their neighbors or village or country. But a man who loves wife and child loves his own flesh. And love for one's own family or clan, as well as loyalty to one's tribe or nation or state or even social class, is nothing other than collective egotism.

Let me speak frankly: I oppose nationalism and patriotism; I oppose the laws of inheritance. I oppose the class rule of the property owners and the class war of the proletariat. I oppose the party system. Why are there armed forces? Why are there courts of law? Why is there a militia? These exist simply for the sake of protecting property, that isolated thing which is detached from all else and which is doomed to death.

We have fallen into a state of disintegration; we have fallen from God. And we will remain lost as long as the deciding factors in our lives remain the covetous will, its struggle for existence, its selfish claims and rights and privileges. The curse that lies over us, this ruined life, has been accepted as normal and even tolerable. We must be freed from the curse of life without spirit and without God!

The natural world around us shows the way to relief. All of life is maintained by the sun, by the air, by water, by the earth and its resources. And to whom was the sun given? To everyone. If there is any one thing that people do have in common, it is the gift of sunlight. But as the early Hutterites said, "If the sun were not hung so high, someone would have claimed it long ago."

And the desire to own property, to take for ourselves things which in no way belong to us, does not stop short at the sun. The air is already bought and sold as a commodity, by health resorts. And what of water? Or waterpower? Why should the earth be parceled out into private hands? Is it any different from the sun? No; the earth belongs to the people who live on it. God intended it for them, but it has been taken over by private individuals. *Pri-*

vare means to steal. Thus private property is stolen property —
property stolen from God and from humankind!

Jesus is the friend of humanity and therefore the enemy of private property. He wants people to have true life. He attacked
the urge to self-preservation and privilege. He gave up everything and became not only the poorest but also the lowest, for
he was classed as a criminal. He kept nothing back for himself.
He had no money of his own: his wandering community had a
common purse.

He said quite plainly that those who follow the urge to self-
preservation are lost. Those who try to keep their life will lose
it. Those who do not leave all that they have cannot come with
me. Sell all that you have and give it away. Keep one coat only,
and give anything beyond that away. If someone asks one hour
of work from you, give two. Do not gather possessions. Do not
hang on to rights and privileges.

Even Nietzsche said that Jesus confronts the false life with a
real life. But what is life? And what is the true life that we should
lead? A body is alive only when all its organs function as one
unit. Life is coherent unity in movement. Life is inseparable from
unity, unity of will, of feeling, and of thought, and cannot exist
apart from it. And humanity will be united only when it is directed by the spirit of community, when each individual works
for the good of all.

If we want community we must want the spirit of community. For this reason I reject the so-called Communist society. My
faith rests solely in that communism that has faith in the Spirit.
The collective soul of community is the Holy Spirit. In this spirit
the church community is unanimous and united, rich in gifts and
powers.

We must remember, however, that just as the unity of the body
cannot be maintained without sacrifice, so the unity of fellowship demands sacrifice if it is to be maintained. If this community
could endure without any sacrifice on the part of its members, it
would be nothing other than the gratification of self. Individuals
in the community must be prepared to sacrifice themselves and
all their powers.

This is true love: that we lay down our lives for our brothers and sisters. And it is the only way to belong to the church. If we grasp this, we will understand the message that is the affirmation of life: not renunciation for the sake of renunciation, but liberation for the sake of new birth — liberation from illusion to reality, from the non-essential to the essential. Then we shall be united at the communal table, as guests at a wedding feast.

— Lecture at the Tolstoy Club, Vienna, November 1929

•

Regarding our relationship to the Religious Socialists: we are very much concerned that the objective proclamation of the kingdom of God not degenerate into some new theoretical orthodoxy. Therefore we agree with you that we must take a lively interest in the socialist and pacifist movements of our day, and we affirm the global conscience they represent — without resorting to their false methods. What we share with them is simply the view that the community of the future will be a life in which all goods are shared freely and lovingly.

— Letter to Professor Evert, Hillsboro, Kansas, 1920

•

We are not simply a society for colonizing, for forming new settlements or villages (as if there weren't enough villages already) where people live as close together and yet as far apart as anywhere else. Nor is it our aim to create a community of the human race or to bring people together for communal living just as they are. That would be a complete failure. All attempts based on the present state of humanity will be unsuccessful. Right from the beginning, they are doomed to go bankrupt.

— Address, October 1933

•

Unless our justice is better than that of the moralists and theologians — and that of the Bolshevists — we cannot enter the kingdom of God. The justice of Bolshevism is inadequate because it does not come from the heart, nor from spiritual fellowship;

it is forced down people's throats. And that is no way to build community.

Bolshevism and political communism are based on an ideal of centralized government and economy. They force a way of life on people. They approach things from without. They tackle the outward problems of economics in the hope of improving inner relationships. But murder is not the way to peace. Killing is not the road to love. Thus Bolshevism is a dangerous abyss; it is anti-Christian. And yet it can point us to something better and purer: Christ and his perfect love.

—Talk, July 1933

•

The basis of our communal life is God and God alone. But we cannot ever say we have acquired this basis, that we now own religion as one owns property. What we have must rather be given to us again each day. It is a dreadful thought, but we can lose it at any time. We are placed on this foundation only by God's grace. Our faith does not result from our natural abilities or wishful thinking. It must be given to us by the Holy Spirit.

—Address, July 1932

WHY WE LIVE IN COMMUNITY

Arnold's own words sum up this essay best: community is not a choice or ideal, but an imperative. And community must be built by the Holy Spirit, or it will fail. Our best instincts may lead us to community, but we will remain incapable of living in community as long as we try to build it with sentimental love or on social ideals. What we need is work — love in action — and faith in God. Work will bring us true joy, and faith in the Spirit will bring us victory over sin.

Life in community is no less than a necessity for us; it is an inescapable "must" that determines everything we do and think.

Yet it is not our good intentions or efforts that have been decisive in our choosing this way of life. Rather, we have been
overwhelmed by a certainty, a certainty that has its origin and
power in the Source of everything that exists. We acknowledge
God as this Source. We must live in community because all life
created by God exists in a communal order and works toward
community.

God is the source of life. On him and through him our common life is built up and led time and again through cataclysmic
struggles to final victory. It is an exceedingly dangerous way, a
way of deep suffering. It is a way that leads straight into the
struggle for existence and the reality of work and into all the
difficulties created by the human character. And yet just this is
our deepest joy: to see clearly the eternal struggle — the inde-
scribable tension between life and death, humankind's position
between heaven and hell — and still to believe in the overwhelming power of life, the power of love to overcome, and the triumph
of truth, because we believe in God.

This faith is not a theory for us; neither is it a dogma, a system
of ideas, or a fabric of words, nor a cult or an organization. Faith
means receiving God himself, being overwhelmed by God. Faith
is the strength that enables us to go this way. It helps us to find
trust again and again when, from a human point of view, the
foundations of trust have been destroyed. Faith gives us the vision
to perceive what is essential and eternal. It gives us the eyes and
hands to see and grasp things which, though everywhere, cannot
otherwise be seen or touched.

If we possess faith, we will no longer judge people in the
light of social custom or according to their weaknesses, for we
will see the lie behind the many masks of our mammonistic
and murderous society. Yet we will not believe either that mali-
ciousness and fickleness, however real, are the ultimate nature of
the human character. Admittedly, in our present nature, without
God, we humans are incapable of community. Temperamental
mood swings, possessive impulses and cravings for physical and
emotional satisfaction, powerful currents of ambition and touchiness, the desire for personal influence over others, and privileges

of all kinds — all these place seemingly insurmountable obstacles in the way of true community. But if we have faith we cannot be deluded into thinking that these realities are decisive: in the face of the power of God and God's all-conquering love, they are of no significance. God is stronger than these realities. The unifying energy of God's Spirit overcomes them all.

It is abundantly clear that the realization of true community, the actual building up of a communal life, is impossible without faith in a higher power. People try again and again to put their trust in human goodness, which really does exist, or in the force of law. But all such efforts are bound to come to grief when faced with the reality of evil. The only power that can build true community is faith in the ultimate good, faith in God.

We must live in community because only through this positive venture will it ever become clear to us how incapable of life human beings are without the life-giving and community-building power of God.

There are political organizations that stand, as we do, for international peace, the abolition of private property, and full community of goods. Yet we cannot simply side with these organizations and fight their battles in their way. We do feel drawn, with them, to all people who suffer need and distress, to those who lack food and shelter and whose very mental development is stunted through exploitation. With them, we stand side by side with the underprivileged, with the degraded and the oppressed. And yet we cannot support the kind of class struggle that employs violent means to avenge exploitation. We reject the defensive wars of the oppressed just as much as we reject the defensive wars of nations.

We must live in community because we have taken our stand in the spiritual fight on the side of all those who fight for freedom, unity, peace, and social justice.

All revolutions, all communes and idealistic or reform-oriented movements, force us to recognize again and again that only one thing can arouse faith in the good: action born of truth. We have only one weapon against the depravity that exists today: the weapon of the Spirit, which is constructive work carried out in the fellowship of love. We do not acknowledge sentimental love, love without work. Nor do we acknowledge dedication to practical work if it does not daily give proof of a heart-to-heart relationship between those who work together, a relationship that comes from the Spirit. The work of love is a matter of the Spirit. The love that comes from the Spirit is work.

When working men and women voluntarily join hands to renounce everything that is self-willed, isolated, or private, their alliances become signposts to the ultimate unity of all people. The will that works toward this unity comes from God. Work as spirit and spirit as work — that is the fundamental nature of the future order of peace, which comes to us in Christ. Work alone makes it possible to live in community, for joy in work means joy in those with whom we work. Such joy is given to us only to the extent that we sustain a consecrated relationship to the eternal, even when performing the most mundane tasks. For everything that is material and earthly is, at the same time, consecrated to God's future.

We must live in community because God wants us to respond to the unclear longings of our time with a clear answer of faith.

The life of love that arises from faith has been witnessed to over the centuries, especially by the Jewish prophets and later by the first Christians. We acknowledge Christ, the historical Jesus, and with him his entire message as proclaimed by his apostles and practiced by his followers. Therefore we stand as brothers and sisters together with all those who have lived in community through the long course of history: the Christians of the first century; the Montanists in the second; the monastics and Arnold of Brescia; the Waldensians; the itinerant followers of Francis of Assisi; the Bohemians and Moravians and the Brothers of the Common Life; the Beguines and Beghards; the Anabaptists of the sixteenth century; the early Quakers; the Labadists of the seventeenth and eighteenth centuries; and many other denominations and movements down to the present day.

We must live in community because we are compelled by the Spirit that leads to community again and again, over the centuries.

We acknowledge Jesus and early Christianity. The early Christians dedicated themselves as much to people's outward needs as to their inner ones. Jesus brought life: he healed sick bodies, resurrected the dead, drove out demons from tormented souls, and carried his message of joy to the poorest of the poor. His message means the realization of the future invisible kingdom now. It is the promise that ultimately the earth will be won wholly for God.

It is the whole that matters here. The love of God does not stop at boundaries or barriers; neither does Jesus stop in the face of property any more than he does in the face of theology, moralism, or the state. Jesus saw into the heart of the rich young man, whom he loved, and said, "One thing you lack: sell all you have, give it to the poor, and come with me!" It was a matter of course for Jesus that his disciples should hold no personal possessions but rather keep a common purse. Only one man was entrusted with the hateful responsibility of managing the disciples' money, and he broke under it — a lesson with no little significance for our mammonistic society today.

Yet even Christ's betrayal and execution did not mean defeat. The Spirit with which the Risen One endowed his itinerant disciples brought forth communal life on a much larger scale. The first church became a community of several thousand people who, because love was burning in them, simply had to live together. In all questions regarding communal life, the forms that emerged were in keeping with an understanding of life as one unified whole.

The first Christians in Jerusalem held everything in common. Whoever owned property felt compelled from within to share it. No one possessed anything that did not belong to the church. Yet what the church owned was there for all. Its generous love excluded no one; its door and heart were closed to no one. At the time of its flowering it found ways to reach all people. And though its members were bound to become the target of hatred and hostility, they still won the love and trust of those closest to them.

The early Christians lived in the Spirit. The Spirit blows like the wind; it is never rigid like iron or stone. The Spirit is infinitely more sensitive and delicate than the inflexible designs of the intellect or the cold, hard framework of governmental or societal structures. The Spirit is more sensitive even than all the emotions of the human soul, more sensitive than all the powers of the human heart, on which people so often try — in vain — to build lasting edifices. Just for this reason the Spirit is also stronger and more irresistible than all these other things. It can never be overcome by any other power, for it is the breadth, depth, and height of being. And it lives on powerfully in Jesus as the inner voice and inner eye that lead to community.

The light of the early church illuminated the path of humankind in only one short flash. Yet its spirit and witness stayed alive even after its members had been murdered and scattered. This happened again and again through history, as various groups of people formed new expressions of the same living Spirit. Witnesses were killed, but new ones were — and are — born to the Spirit again and again. Communities pass away. But the church that creates them remains.

Efforts to organize community artificially can result only in ugly, lifeless caricatures. But when we are empty, when we open ourselves to the Living One, to the Holy Spirit, we will experience the same life as did the early Christians. This Spirit is joy in the Living One, joy in God as the only real life. It is joy in all people, because all people have life from God. This Spirit drives us to all people and brings us joy in living and working for one another, for it is the spirit of creativity and love.

Community life is possible only when we surrender to this Spirit. This is such a powerful experience that we may never feel equal to it; in truth, we never will. But our energies can be quickened by its white-hot heat, and if we allow it to burn us to the core, to the point of sacrifice, its flames will radiate far and wide. Community life is martyrdom by fire: it means the daily sacrifice of all our strength and all our rights, all the supposedly justified claims we commonly make on life. As individual logs we must be burned away, must be united in glowing flames, if we want to send warmth and light out into the land.

We must live in community because the spirit of joy and love gives us such an urge to reach out to others that we wish to be united with them for all time.

The whole of natural life is a parable of God's future community. Just as the air surrounds us or as a blowing wind engulfs us, we need to be immersed in the blowing Spirit who unites and renews everything. Just as water washes and cleanses us every day, so in baptism we must witness to our purification from everything that is of death. This "burial" in water must signify a complete break from the status quo. It must be a vow of mortal enmity toward all evil within us and around us. And the raising of ourselves up out of the water must proclaim resurrection in vivid imagery and unforgettable clarity.

The resurrection we see everywhere in nature is no different: after the dying of autumn and winter comes the blossoming of spring and the fruit-bearing of summer; after seedtime comes harvest. In fact, the whole course of human history, from our origins to our final fulfillment, is symbolized by the cycle of nature.

Symbolism can be found in the trivialities of existence, too: when approached with reverence, even daily rites such as mealtimes can become consecrated festivals of community. On a deeper level, we can find expression of community in the symbol of the Lord's Supper: the meal of wine and bread. The Meal of Remembrance not only witnesses to the catastrophe of Christ's death and to his second coming, but also to the fact that we receive him in ourselves. It witnesses to his church, his body, as the ultimate unity of life.

In the human body, community is maintained only by the constant cycle of cells dying and being replaced by new ones. In a similar way, a life of full community can exist only where there is heroic sacrifice. Because it is an educational fellowship of mutual help and correction, of shared resources, and of work, true community is a covenant made in voluntary surrender and sacrifice. As such it fights for the existence of the church.

In the context of church community, justice has nothing to do with satisfying even reasonable demands for personal rights; on the contrary, it consists in surrendering everything to God. This cannot come about through hard demands made on others, however, but in joyous self-sacrifice, for God's Spirit comes to expression as cheerful and voluntary work.

We love the body because it is a consecrated dwelling place
of the Spirit. We love the soil because God created it to be cultivated by the communal work of humankind. We love physical
work, the work of muscle and hand, and we love the craftsman's
art, in which the spirit guides the hand. We see the mystery of
community in the way spirit and hand work through each other.

We love the activity of mind and spirit, too: the richness of
all the creative arts and the intellectual and spiritual exploration
of history and humanity. Whatever our work, we must recognize
and do the will of God in it. And God has entrusted the earth to
us not only as an inheritance but also as a task: our garden must
become God's garden, and our work must further God's work.

We must live in community because we are stimulated by
the Spirit who calls nature, work, and culture to unity and
community with God.

No less significant than the symbol of the body is the symbol
of community as the harbinger of God's kingdom. Where God
reigns there will be joy and peace and justice. In the same way
that every body consists of millions of independent cells, so millions of people will become one organism. This organism exists
already today as the invisible church.

When we acknowledge as reality the unity and order of this
invisible church, we acknowledge at the same time the freedom
of the Spirit within it. The more clearly a community defines its
unique task, the more deeply conscious it must be of belong-
ing to the *una sancta,* the One Church. Because it is part of a
larger organism, it needs the give-and-take that comes from serving the whole body, and it needs to be instructed and guided by
the united witness of all those who believe in the church.

The secret of community is to be found in the freedom of self-
determination, in the personal decision of the individual members
to surrender to the whole and, at the same time, to exercise
their will for the good. This freedom, without which communal
life cannot exist, is not a matter of power exercised by human
self-will, nor is it a matter of spinelessness or unrestraint. In a
community of deeply moved people who believe in the Spirit, the
freedom of the individuals lives in their free decision for the will

of the Spirit. Working from within each member as the will for the good, freedom becomes unanimity and concord. The will of a person liberated in this way will be directed toward the kingdom, toward God's unity, and toward the good of the whole human race. As such it will be vital and intensely energetic.

Standing as it does in a world of death an active will must constantly assert itself against the destructive and enslaving powers of lying, impurity, capitalism, and military force. It is engaged in battle everywhere: against the spirit of murder, against all hostility (including the venom of the taunting, quarrelling tongue), and against all the wrong and injustice people do to each other. It must fight in public as well as in private life against the very nature of hatred and death, and against all that opposes community.

The call to freedom is a call to battle without pause. Those who are called to it must be continually alert. They need not only the greatest willpower they themselves can muster, but also the aid of God, in order to meet the plight of the oppressed, to stand with the poor, and to fight against all evil in themselves and in the world around them.

This fight must be waged more strongly against the evil within a community than against the evil of the world outside. Most importantly, it must be fought within each individual, who must take up the fight against the old Adam from the position of the new. In this way all softness and all flabby indulgence will be overcome by the burning power of love.

We must live in community because the struggle of life against death demands united ranks of souls and bodies.

Community of goods presupposes the willingness of the individual members to turn over unconditionally to the common household whatever they acquire in the way of income or property, large or small. Yet even the community does not regard itself as the corporate owner of its inventory and enterprises. Rather, it acts as a trustee of the assets it holds for the common good of all, and for this reason it keeps its door open to all. By the same token it requires for its decision-making undisturbed unanimity in the Spirit.

The struggle for unity and for love is fought on many fronts with many different weapons. So too, the work of community will find expression in many different ways. But we must have certainty of purpose for every stretch of the way we are called to go, and when we possess this certainty we will be given the strength for loyalty and unerring clarity, even in small things, to the very end. There can be no great commission without a clearly defined task. Only those who stand firm can bear the standard. Nothing can be entrusted to the person who cannot hold out.

It is of decisive importance that our work lead only to Christ, that it serve the whole, the church, the coming kingdom. When we see our task as something special in itself, we will go astray. But when we serve the whole, we serve God and the community. Before our human service can become divine service, however, we must recognize how small and limited it is in the face of the whole.

A special calling — living in community, for instance — must never be confused with the church of Christ itself. Life in community means discipline in community, education in community, and continual training for the discipleship of Christ. Yet the mystery of the church is something different from this, something far greater. It is God's life, and coming from God it penetrates community. This penetration of the divine into the human occurs whenever the tension of desperate yearning produces an openness and readiness in which God alone may act and speak. At such moments a community can be commissioned by the invisible church and given certainty for a specific mission: to speak and act in the name of the church, albeit without mistaking itself for the church.

The church we acknowledge lives in the Holy Spirit. The Spirit in which we believe bears the church within itself. This church of the Spirit will give life to the future unity of humankind. It gives life already now to all truly living communities. The foundation and basic element of every community is not merely the combination of its members but simply and solely the unity of the Holy Spirit, for the true church is present there.

An organism becomes a unit through the unity of conscious-

ness brought about by the spirit that animates it. It is the same
in a believing community. The future unity of humankind, when
God alone will rule, is ensured by the Holy Spirit. For this Spirit
is the coming leader and Lord himself. The only thing we can
hold on to here and now, the only thing we can already perceive
of this great future of love and unity, is the Spirit. Faith in the
Spirit is faith in the church and faith in the kingdom.

In the life of a community, several decisive questions will need
to be confronted again and again. How are we called? To what
are we called? Will we follow the call? Only a few at a time will
be called to the special way that is ours. And those who are called
must hold to the common task shown them by God for the rest
of their lives. They must be ready to sacrifice life itself for the
sake of unity.

People tear themselves away from home, parents, and career
for the sake of marriage; they risk their lives for the sake of
wife and child. In the same way it is necessary to break away
and sacrifice everything for the sake of this way. Our witness to
voluntary community of goods and work, to a life of peace and
love, will have meaning only when we throw our entire life and
livelihood into it.

It is now [1925] over five years since our tiny fellowship in
Berlin decided to venture, in the sense of this confession, to live
and work together in community on the basis of trust. With
time, a life of total community came into being. We are small
in number, and we come from the most diverse backgrounds and
walks of life, but we want to place ourselves as one movement
in the service of all people. Given our basis of faith, we cannot
approach the development of our community from a purely economic point of view. We cannot simply select the most capable
people for our various work departments. We aim for efficiency
in all areas; but far more important, we seek faith. All of us —
whether committed member, helper, or guest, and no matter
what our task — must ask ourselves daily whether or not we are
growing into the coming community ruled by Christ.

Our work, then, is a venture dared again and again. Yet we
are not its driving force; rather, it is we who are driven and who

must be urged on. The danger of exhaustion and uselessness is always present, but it will be continually overcome by the faith that underlies mutual help.

— Essay, 1925

•

It is certainly true that God works in people, in men and in women. But when this truth is exaggerated to the point where we believe solely in ourselves and other human beings, we are on the wrong track. We must believe in God in such a way that not we but God is in the center. Only then can God work in us and through us. We must become so transparent that what other people see is no longer us, but God. Community can come into being in no other way. No matter how humble, dedicated, or unassuming we may be, we cannot build community in our own strength.

— Talk with visitors, June 1933

•

We have nothing. If we ever thought we had community, we have now seen that we do not have it. And it is good for us to have seen that. Community exists exclusively in Christ and his life-giving Spirit. If we forget him and are left without his influence, if we forfeit his working among us, it is all over with our community.

— Address, November 1935

•

Our communism of goods, of table, of work, and of life should never take the place of what is essential, even if all these things have sprung out of the essential. The only essential is God: God's will for complete love, God's power for renewed life, and God's Spirit for active brotherhood.

— Letter, 1927

8

The Fight against Mammon

All his life, Arnold fought against mammonism, that is, "the enslavement of the soul to circumstance." This fight was not lessened even by a life of poverty. His children remember that their mother would occasionally bring up her worries about financial debts at breakfast, the one time of day when the family might have relaxed. Arnold's response was predictable: "Emmy, worry is also mammonism. Let's spend time with the children."

GOD OR MAMMON

"No one can serve two masters. Either he will hate the one and love the other, or he will be devoted to the one and look down on the other. You cannot serve God and mammon." This great and dynamic struggle of which Jesus spoke is still raging today. *Mamona* was the Aramaic word for wealth, and with it, Satan tempted even Jesus: "I will give you all this if you will fall down and worship me."

In the early Christian era, some scholars interpreted "Mammon" as a name of the devil Beelzebub. Others interpreted it as the name of a demon particularly connected with money. Any attempt to combine service to God and service to mammon will end in failure. We must cleave to God alone and despise mammon!

God and mammon are the two masters between whom we

must choose. They are two goals that cannot be reconciled. The pursuit of money, the preoccupation with outward things, is incompatible with all other goals and purposes. Devoting ourselves to a life of ease and pleasure means letting outward things become the determining force in our lives. Serving mammon means secretly worshiping things, clinging to them and loving them to the exclusion of God.

Materialistic people demand everything for themselves. They are carried away by their senses and seek nothing but bodily ease, comfort, and pleasure. They value things and not people and are dominated by their power. They have been made slaves to them and have been deprived of the wealthy life that gives and bestows. They ask only what life can give to them; they know only rights and not responsibilities. Their uppermost goal is payment and gain. They strive to secure property and comfort at the expense of others. Believers, however, see in this love of money the old — and ever new — danger that threatened even the first Christians.

Nothing but overcoming the self can rid us of the false, debasing life that serves mammon. Even nonbelievers recognize this. Nietzsche said, "Consume yourself in your own flame; how can you become new unless you first turn to ashes?" And Goethe wrote, "As long as you've not learned / to die and live again, / you're just a gloomy guest / here on this dark earth."

But how is it possible to "re-become," as the mystic Eckhart demanded; how can one, in Goethe's words, "de-self oneself" when one is bound and fettered as mammon's slave? How can one enter a strong man's house and steal his goods, unless the strong man is bound first?

When a strong man guards his own dwelling his goods are left in peace; but if someone stronger comes and conquers him, the spoil is soon divided. And Jesus is stronger than mammon: he has overcome, disarmed, and bound the enemy. The cross is stronger than the devil. Its victory is deliverance from mammon, from the deadness of a debased life. If we die with Christ, we shall live with him. Therefore, "Set your hearts on what is above, not on what is on earth. For you have died, and your life is now hidden in Christ."

— Essay, 1915

THE FIGHT AGAINST MAMMON

If life is love, and love means fellowship, and if all living things interact to promote life and unity and freedom, then how is it possible that death, destruction, and murder are so rampant in the world today?

Two powers are at work in the world: the power of love that leads people to associate with each other, and the power of death that separates people and destroys the fellowship of love. This power of death poisons the organism of humanity, making it sick and corrupt. It murders and kills. It covets and isolates. It attacks all that holds life together. It destroys the coherence of all living things. But alongside this power that murders and enslaves, a constructive and creative power is still at work.

This tension between opposites is a reality of life. People who try to consecrate their lives or devote themselves to a cause must face this either/or, this question of God or mammon. And it is not true that everything religious is united against everything irreligious. It would be nearer the truth to draw the dividing line through both.

Not all who call themselves Christians are connected to the same center, nor are they motivated by the same thing. The religion of many who confess to the name of Jesus Christ has nothing to do with God or the coming kingdom. Their religion is really that of the Anti-god; it is permeated by the demonic powers of the abyss that cause the disintegration of human solidarity.

Is not the great world organization that names itself after Christ serving a god other than the God whom Jesus confessed? Has not the institutional church sided with wealth and protected it; sanctified mammon, christened warships, and blessed soldiers going to war? Has not this church in essence denied him whom it confesses? Is not the Christian state the most ungodly institution that ever existed? And are not the state and the organized church, which protect privilege and wealth, diametrically opposed to what is to come: God's new order?

Nobody can serve two masters. Nobody can serve God and mammon. The message of Christ had to do with the "transvaluation of all values" — the coming kingdom of God. His first witnesses testified to a radically new order, an order concealed from those blinded by the god of this world. This god — the god of greed and murderous possessiveness — stands opposed to the kingdom of justice, unity, and love. Jesus defined its nature with utmost sharpness. He called Satan the "murderer from the beginning."

Even the blind can see that economic development means the murder of thousands of people, that big business rules through the power of the lying spirit, and that governments wage war by means of deception. A capitalistic society can be maintained only by lies; if people were to recognize this, there would be a total revolt against the greatest deception in the history of humankind. But we are a long way from revolting. Most pious and even many working people think, "Rich and poor have to be." They ignore the fact that it is impossible to amass any kind of fortune without cheating, without depriving and hurting others and destroying their lives. They fail to realize that big business, concentrated in a few hands, can steer hundreds of thousands toward certain ruin through unemployment.

Why do these facts remain hidden from us? How is it possible to be cheated of justice and be blind to it? It is because we ourselves are also under the rule of this god, mammon.

Mammon is the rule of money over people. It means dependence on income and finances instead of on God. We recognize that mammon is the enemy of God, but we cannot apply the lever that lifts it off its hinges: we ourselves are so dominated by it that we lack the strength to rebel.

The deepest human relationships are based not on mammon, but the spirit. No one of us can live in isolation; we are all interdependent. All of us are interrelated in groups, families, classes, and trade unions; in nations, states, churches, and all kinds of associations. And through our humanity we are interrelated in an even deeper way: through the love of God that flows from spirit to spirit and heart to heart, leading to organic, constructive fellowship.

But there is a devilish means that seeks to rob us of heart and

spirit and God. This means is money. Money reduces human relationships to materialistic associations. It destroys the highest
human goals. At first it may be just a means of barter, but later
it becomes a commodity in itself. It becomes power. In the end,
it destroys all true fellowship.

Money and love are mutually exclusive. Where mammon
rules, the possessive will is stronger than the will to community.
The struggle to survive becomes stronger than the spirit of mutual
help. Where mammon rules, matter is stronger than spirit, and
self-assertion stronger than solidarity. Mammon never motivates
people to work in a creative way for a life of fellowship. Instead,
it engenders the enslavement of the soul to circumstance. It is
the spirit of lying, impurity, and murder, the spirit of weakness
and death.

Jesus, the prince of life, declared war on this spirit, and we
must declare war on it too. When our inmost eye has been
opened to his light, it can no longer respond to what mammon
demands. When our hearts are set on the future, when we expect God's kingdom, we can no longer accumulate property. We
will turn our backs on everything present and live instead for
freedom, unity, and peace.

Jesus entered the temple with a whip not to strike people, but
to show his contempt for money: his Father's house belonged to
God, not to mammon. In the Gospel of Matthew, he exhorted
the otherwise blameless rich youth to confirm his love by selling everything: "Give all you have to the poor, and come follow
me." And when he was shown the coin of the emperor, he answered, "Give to Caesar what belongs to Caesar, and to God
what belongs to God."

This attack on the order of mammon resulted in his death. Yet
life had the final victory. The men and women who had gathered around him in life waited for something new after his death.
They waited for the Spirit. They knew that the spirit of love,
order, and freedom was the spirit of God's kingdom. And this
Spirit came upon them, bringing about a church: a fellowship of
work and goods in which everything belonged to all, in which all
were active to the full extent of their powers and gifts.

This church succumbed to the process that destroys life. Just as individuals die, so this church also died. But in the course of the centuries a new church rose. Time and again small communities were formed in which men and women declared war on mammon and took upon themselves the poverty of generosity. In choosing this poverty, they chose the richest way.

Simple communism existed among primitive people. And throughout history the revolutionary struggle, the fight against materialism, has continued. We who see the appalling results of capitalism today stand at the point where the uprising against capitalism begins. The words of Jesus — "He who is not with me is against me" — hold true also for us. We are on the same side as all revolutionaries who fight against mammon.

There are two ways to fight against mammon. One holds to the ideals of socialism and communism. The other is the way of communal work and fellowship in all things spiritual and material, the voluntary gathering of those who are free of private property and capital. This is the seed that sprouts in the stony field.

At first, just a little tip of grass shows. After a few days of sun and rain, there are patches of living green. And then, only weeks later, the whole field is flourishing with life. In spite of weeds and stones, the young crop has broken through. What the individual blade of grass cannot achieve, the whole field can. The harvest is there!

But wheat and weeds cannot be separated before the harvest. We must wait for harvest time, otherwise the wheat will be torn out and the weeds left standing. It would be completely contrary to the Spirit of Jesus to hang the servants of mammon on lampposts in bloody revolution. We can have no part in violent revolution because it allies itself with the father of lies.

It is self-deception to think we can overcome mammon by violence, for violence is of the same evil spirit as mammon. We cannot drive out poison by means of poison. The new can be born only of the new; only out of life comes life; only of love can love be born. Only out of the will to community can community arise.

And community is alive wherever small bands of people meet, ready to work for the one great goal, to belong to the one true future. Already now we can live in the power of this future; already now we can shape our lives in accordance with God and God's kingdom. The kingdom of love, which is free of mammon, is drawing near. Change your thinking radically so that you will be ready for the coming order!

—Lecture, 1923

9

God with Us

How do we come to Jesus? To experience the heart of God we need Jesus; to experience Jesus, we need to experience that moment in which he sacrificed his heart. And that was the moment when he sealed the surrender of his life with the last drop of his blood, when his eyes dimmed and his heart broke — the hour when he also comforted a criminal. It was Golgotha: that time and place in which we enter into pure, unclouded fellowship with God's eternity, God's heart, God's love. Golgotha is the window through which we can look from this darkened earth into the radiance of God's heart.

"If Christ were born a thousand times in Bethlehem but not in you, you would still be lost eternally." That is what the mystery of religion witnesses to: the uniting of the individual soul with Jesus Christ; the uniting of the individual spirit with the universal Spirit at one moment in time.

—Lecture, March 1921

THE EXPERIENCE OF GOD

In this excerpt from Innerland, *Arnold stresses Christ as a person, not a concept or a merely historical figure. Jesus did not bring a new religion, but new life. And his message is meaningless if it does not affect the way we live.*

The kingdom of God is the will of God made real. And God's will is unconditional; it cannot be restricted. It does not acknowledge any other will and tolerates no rival authority. Nor does it ally itself with anything that curtails, restricts, or limits love. The kingdom of God is power: it is the righteousness of God, the peace of Jesus Christ, and joy in the Holy Spirit.

And God's kingdom can begin already now, in our time, wherever the peace of Christ reigns. For God sends the Spirit of his Son into our hearts. This brings both obligation and authority: those gripped by this Spirit must drive away all other spirits, and must establish as valid the spiritual laws of the kingdom even in the outer spheres of life.

God's peace within our hearts will enable us to become builders and bearers of outward peace. For God fills the believing heart with such overflowing joy that it must go out in love to all, driving away the spirits of war and strife, of competition and private property. Those who receive this joy will be drawn, one after the other, into the circle of love and complete community. The spirit of the church is the spirit of God's kingdom, the spirit of justice, peace, and joy. And it is the church of Jesus Christ that brings this kingdom down to earth here and now.

The Spirit of God works within our hearts, but it brings about outward consequences as well. It wants community in everything, and so it tears down all existing human relationships and builds them up anew. This spirit does not originate with people, but is poured into believing hearts — hearts which, when filled with God, radiate a faith that strengthens life and increases works a thousandfold. This faith is something personal, and yet it is also objective. It is the confident trust with which Paul declares: "I live, yet it is no longer I who live, but Christ who lives in me; the life I live now in the flesh I live by faith in the Son of God." There can be no life of faith other than that lived in unity and community with Christ.

Faith is made alive in Christ. We live in Christ, and Christ lives in us; it is he who transforms our lives from within. Luther experienced this mutual relationship only after years of struggle; for this reason, his experience of God is of historical importance. His consciousness of sin and his fear before God's justice threw him into such agony that he did not know which way to turn. He could find no consolation, either from within or from without, and felt he must perish utterly.

Only through the grace of Christ's love could he later affirm, writing to his friend Spenlein, that Christ justifies us without our own efforts or works, and that without this justification, we cannot live before God, before ourselves, or before others:

> Learn to know Christ, that is, the crucified Christ.... Say to him: "You, Lord Jesus, are my righteousness, but I am your sin. You have taken upon yourself what was mine and given me what was yours; you have accepted what you have not been, and given me what I have not been." Yes, you will learn from Christ himself that, in the same way as he has accepted you, he has made your sins his and his righteousness yours.

This mutual relationship, this receiving and giving of one to the other, is Luther's understanding of the words: "It is no longer I who live, but Christ who lives in me." And the certainty of this oneness depends not on us, but on him. We die to ourselves only when our will becomes one with his will to die. Everything we have ever been or experienced or achieved must die at the cross. Only from Christ's grave can the will be resurrected into freedom.

It is the loneliness of the Crucified One that gives us freedom from self-importance. It is the step taken by faith, into death and through the grave, that leads to certainty of life. Christ accepts us so completely that he says, "I am this poor sinner; his sin is my sin, and his death is my death." This unity in death frees us from sin, despite the most terrifying consciousness of it. We have life in the Risen One!

Now Christ is in us: he has taken our lives upon himself. Our old lives are taken away; through his life, we now share all that he is. Everything he possesses he now offers to us. The same Jesus who says, "All power in heaven and on earth has been given to me" now gives us his authority. The same Christ who takes as his own the seat at the right hand of the Father makes us partakers in his divinity. He, the Son of Man, the last Adam, has made us his brothers and sisters.

People often forget that for Luther, faith meant taking hold of the precious and costly treasure itself, that is, Christ. Only Christ himself could give substance and content to Luther's faith. But we need not define faith; what we need is simply Christ. Christ comes down to us and becomes our life. His coming is faith; what he does is faith. With all their understanding and good intentions, the human forces of piety, wisdom, and religion have no faith. Their efforts to rise up to God are futile. Believing in Christ means quite simply that Christ becomes one with us. It means that he abides in us. The life we have in faith is Christ himself.

And where Christ is, the law that condemns us is forever canceled. Here is Christ, who condemns sin and throttles death! Where he is, everything that destroys life must withdraw. Who shall separate us from the love of Christ? Christ is here! No power can sever us from the love of God as long as he, the most powerful, is our master. If we lose him, there is no help, no consolation, no counsel anywhere. The terror of death will be all there is to know. But to be with Christ means life and peace, within and without.

The life of Christ is energy, for God is dynamic power. Luther says expressly that the Holy Spirit does not leave a believer idle, but impels him to "all manner of good, in which he can exercise his faith and prove his Christian character." But here we must go beyond Luther, for here he goes no further.

If Christ lives in us, he will unfold his powers in us. The justice and righteousness of his Father will become our justice and righteousness. Christ in us means serving others and working for others, for our faith must be as active in love as was his. What he accomplished, we must represent in deed as well.

The unity of Jesus with the Father is so complete that he says, "What is mine is thine, and what is thine is mine." In the same way, believers are so united with Christ that they too can say, to Christ and their brothers and sisters, "Mine is thine, and thine mine." The love of Christ impels them to act and live in this way. The justice and righteousness of Christians is Christ and his life.

The Holy Spirit urges them toward the same good deeds that Jesus did.

Those gripped by Jesus have, like him, a love that relinquishes all privileges. When they confess that Christ is their life, like Christ they choose voluntary poverty for the sake of love; like Christ they sacrifice their lives unconditionally for friend and foe, with all they are and have.

Jesus was given all power and might. His love, therefore, must rule unconditionally and unhindered in the lives of those who receive his authority. Only then can he give them his commission. And this commission must fill the whole of life. It must transform all circumstances and relationships in accordance with its objective demands.

We should not say that we believe in Christ and his kingdom, or in unity and community with him, if we do not sacrifice everything and share everything with one another, just as he did. We should not claim that his goodness and his righteousness have become our goodness and our righteousness if we do not give ourselves to the poor and oppressed just as he gave himself to them. We should not think we have experienced the Strong One, who exercises all authority at the right hand of the Power, if his works of justice and community are not fulfilled in our lives. If we have faith, the working of this faith must become obvious in works of perfect love. If Christ rules in us, his rule must go out from us into all lands. If his spirit is in us, streams of his spirit must transform everything around us in accord with his promises about the coming kingdom.

— Innerland

•

Deeds reveal the character of the heart. If the heart is not clear and undivided — "single," as Jesus puts it — then it is weak, flabby, and indolent, incapable of accepting God's will, of making important decisions, or of taking strong action. This is why Jesus attached the greatest significance to singleness of heart, to simplicity, unity, solidarity, and decisiveness. Purity of heart is nothing else than absolute integrity, which can overcome desires that enervate and divide. Determined single-heartedness is what the heart needs in order to be receptive, truthful and upright, confident and brave, firm and strong.

— *Innerland*

THE SPIRIT OF THE RISEN ONE

Christian circles have often been attacked on account of their call to repentance. They are told that the unceasing accusation of the conscience paralyzes initiative, takes away freedom, and destroys personality. Certainly one would have to come to this conclusion if one were to experience only the consciousness of sin by itself. But those who proclaim Christ cannot separate repentance from faith. The message of the cross is inseparably one with the proclamation of the Risen One.

Luther called for daily remorse and repentance because he experienced again and again the unconditional certainty of possessing the gift of salvation. He knew that no one could accuse or condemn God's elect, and he knew himself to be justified by God himself. He had experienced the presence of the Christ who intercedes for us with the very powers of his resurrected life.

One of the things that cannot easily be explained is that for a Christian, the deepest recognition of sin and absolute freedom from all condemnation must become completely one. The source of inner freedom and faith lies in God and Christ, while the murky depths of remorse and repentance are found only in ourselves.

It is the soul's instinct of self-preservation which holds us back from complete honesty about our own moral condition. Without the strength of the Gospel, unrestrained insight into our own helplessness and depravity would lead us to despair, for it is just when we attempt to apply the strictest self-discipline and the firmest moral code that we are faced with the absolute impossibility of justifying ourselves in the eyes of God. The Gospel wants the truth about our condition to come completely out into the open. At the same time, it offers us the possibility of a clear and joyful conscience, a merciful God in the midst of deepest self-recognition. What we are unable to do by our own efforts, God has done: He sent us his Son.

Faith in this fact cannot be shaken by anything. Even though all people speak against us, even though they accuse and condemn us, we believers in God and in Christ still cannot be discouraged. However hard the times, however low the ebb of moral and religious power, this one fact remains: God gave his own Son for us. And even if we cannot find other people who in their actual lives reflect God's nature, still Jesus remains — the redemption for every person.

This historical fact must become the spiritual experience of the present. It means that God, in giving us Jesus, gave us everything. Perfect love became flesh, and this means his love will become life and reality everywhere. Once we grasp this we can no longer despair of God's love or question God's intervention on our behalf. However, we misuse and belittle the certainty of this love if we accept it without at the same time destroying our own vanity and self-will. The collapse of national pride, self-accusation, and guilt, the disintegration of cultural values in state and church, and the repeated evidence that it is impossible to produce with purely human powers the conditions of peace and justice we long for: all these experiences convince us that we need grace.

Grace is a sovereign gift; we can do nothing to acquire it. That inner state in which it seems everything is breaking down is the preparation we need to receive Christ. Only when everyone accuses us, only when we condemn ourselves in the sharpest way, are we in a condition of inner readiness for the message of salvation.

The invincible power of the first Christians sprang from the fact that they believed in the presence of that same Christ who had ascended to the Father. We, too, can believe in the powers of Jesus' death and the strength of his resurrection only when we experience the immediate presence of Christ.

The first Christians lived by the promise of the Risen One: "I am with you always, even to the end of the world." All their meetings were permeated by this certain faith; they believed in and experienced his personal presence so strongly that they lived entirely under his influence. The awareness of Jesus' presence was the secret of their strength. They experienced the Risen One as the Spirit present among them. Through him they were freed from all bondage, and through him they were freed to use all their human gifts and powers.

For us, too, faith in the Risen One and in his Spirit must lead to a new attitude in everyday life. And faith unlocks the spiritual powers at work in Christ. The Lord is Spirit, and he molds our lives according to his image. How we actually live, how we put love into action, depends not on moral conviction but on faith. Everything depends on whether we know the resurrected Christ and whether we have his Spirit. It does not help us to long for Christ to appear from heaven. The only way to truly experience his presence is to know and feel in our hearts that the Christ, who was raised from the dead by God, has come to us as the living word.

—Essay, 1919

•

The call to repentance by the prophets and by John the Baptist is this call: Let your hearts be moved, for mighty things are in store for you! The movement that John speaks of is love, the movement of the heart of God. Unless our hearts are moved, they will remain cold. And when our hearts are cold, we think and talk about our own personal weaknesses and those of others, because our hearts are not moved by the greatest love of all. God is love. When we live in his love, we are freed from all petty thoughts.

—Talk, July 1933

THE LIVING WORD

Without God's calling, no one can proclaim the word, for the gospel is living power, not a dead letter. For the New Testament given by the Holy Spirit is written not with ink on paper, but by God's finger upon our hearts. The scribes whose hearts are not filled with God can preach the printed word as servants of the Old Testament, but never as servants of the Spirit. Everything depends on their vocation, for unless God has called them, they cannot proclaim the meaning of scripture. Even if their interpretation is true, their teaching will be in vain if God is not in it.

God does not talk to those whom he has not called. Such persons have gotten up too early; the sun has not yet risen for them. They have started on their way at night. They have gone without being sent. Without a light, they thresh empty straw, and their sword slashes at the wind. God has not commanded them. God has not called them. Neither, then, can they be God's witnesses. Therefore their speech has no incisiveness, no power, no spirit, and makes no impression; their talking does not bear the fruit of life.

There is a great and powerful difference between serving the letter and serving the Spirit. The one excludes the other. Those who serve the letter read from scripture only what is contained in the written word. They sit in Moses' chair. They proclaim not the scripture, but the words that hold it.

Those who serve the Spirit do something completely different. They serve the gospels by proclaiming the Holy Spirit, who sows, plants, and inscribes Christ in people's hearts. They speak by inspiration of the Holy Spirit; they are appointed by the authority of the Holy Spirit. They speak not in their own strength, but as the mouth of God. Only through people kindled by the Holy Spirit does God give light.

Servants of the Spirit must be appointed by the Spirit. They must be chosen, called, and sent out by the Holy Spirit, and equally, of course, by a people filled with this spirit. They are sent out into the harvest by God himself and by the church. Christ himself was sent and anointed by this Spirit. The apostles could not go out as servants of the word until they were clothed with power from on high, by the living word proclaimed through the living Bible. That is why their words have such force, such clarity, and such power. That is why their sayings cut like a knife, stabbing the heart and piercing the marrow.

To preach Christ and to proclaim his gospel means to impart the Holy Spirit: to plant in people's hearts the word and to awaken them to a new birth through the Holy Spirit. It means representing the Spirit in such a way that the enemies of God are beside themselves because of it. Just as the apostles met this resistance, so should all other servants of the Spirit meet the same resistance. For God does not change; God has grown neither greater nor less since the time of the apostles.

Therefore each of us should examine our calling and see whether we are servants of the Spirit or of the cold and dead letter. We each must ask ourselves whether the Holy Spirit goes with us in our service and whether our preaching brings forth fruit, or whether it is empty, as it is with every servant of the letter.

Christ sends out his own like the Father sent him: to bear fruit. He arms them with the same authority with which he is armed and says of them: "Those who believe in me will do all that I do, and even more." Those whose word is not imbued with the power of Christ should therefore know that they have not been called as servants of the Spirit or of the living word. They should know that they have crept in among the sheep as thieves and as murderers. They are like one who carries water to the Rhine (which has enough water already) while ignoring the needs of the thirsty.

Only those who are of God speak God's word. In the same way, only those who are of God hear God's word. And God speaks to the children of his Spirit in a special language. They alone understand God, and if others come near to listen, they understand nothing. For the secret of God's language is love, not the love that comes from human beings, but from God. Peter was not allowed to go to the flock until he was asked whether he loved and until he had received the Holy Spirit.

The apostles waited for this love just as they waited for the Spirit. Until they had received it, they did not dare preach a word. They knew that without this love, the Holy Spirit would not go with them on their journeying. With it, they would know what to do and where to go.

Those who are led by love will wait on God at all times. It is not enough if they wait for God's calling at certain moments.

No, they must be made the mouth, hand, and instrument of God every single day of their lives. They must be protected so that they do not understand or speak in their own strength, but do and say all things in God. They must not speak until God has told them what to say, nor must they speak when it is too late, when God has already left them.

— Address, September 1933

•

We believe that every human being has a longing for true justice, true love and unity. Therefore, the open door of the community is open to everyone. At the same time we realize that not all of us are ready for community at every stage of our lives. You can't expect everyone to be able to accept it at every moment. For example, I can't simply stand at the Leipzigerstrasse in Berlin and call, "Come here, all of you, come and live at the Bruderhof!" It is not cowardice that keeps us from doing this. It would be folly; many people would simply not be in the position to understand such a call. They would not be mature enough in their inner development to follow it. God must call them first. I have no right to call anyone unless the Spirit himself has already called that person.

— Talk, October 1933

•

There can be no victory of the Spirit as long as people set themselves up as healers of sickness. The Holy Spirit has nothing to do with magic. Not until all human claims disappear will the Spirit of Jesus Christ show himself as the Spirit who heals sickness, drives out demons, and overcomes death. Not until we lay down our self-will can God be victorious over demons....

Christ reveals himself only to those who no longer seek their own honor and greatness. He seeks that church in which people are unimportant, in which people have become like children and beggars. He reveals himself only to the church that lives without hypocrisy and without any religious show. But there, where people turn to him for all things, demons and darkness will yield.

— Talk, June 1935

10

The Church Comes Down to Us

Arnold always emphasized Gemeinde *(the living congregation of believers) over* Kirche *(the church as an institution or establishment). He believed that the true church transcends time and space, uniting all those who call on God and receive his Spirit. Thus the church is past and present and future, and lives on earth as well as in heaven. For him, the high point of the ecclesiastical year was Pentecost: the celebration of the outpouring of the Holy Spirit as the foundation of the "living church."*

The following address, a response to a letter from his friend the Swiss Religious Socialist Leonhard Ragaz, touches on these themes. Ragaz had asked whether Arnold's community, the Bruderhof, considered itself to be "the" church, as opposed to just one of many other members in the "family of Christ." The question, Ragaz conceded, was a delicate one: "If such a great thing would be given to you, should you not handle it with the utmost reserve, as a miracle which could easily withdraw, something of which you were not worthy, as none of us is?"

Arnold considered Ragaz's question carefully, dedicating three evenings to the topic; the excerpt below summarizes these discussions.

It is of decisive importance that we remember the mission of the church as it is laid upon us in the outpouring of the Holy Spirit. If anyone asks us whether we, a few weak and needy people living in community, are "the" church, we have to say, No, we are not. Like all human beings, however, we are the recipients of God's love. And like everyone else — more so, if anything — we are unworthy and unfit for the work of the Holy Spirit, for the building of the church, and for its mission to the world.

But if anyone asks, "Does the church of God come down to you?" then we have to answer yes. For the church comes down wherever believers are gathered who have no other will but that God's kingdom come and that the church of Jesus Christ be revealed. The church is wherever the Holy Spirit is.

Of course, we need to call on God if we want to receive the Holy Spirit; willpower by itself is not enough, for it remains rooted in what is human. The Holy Spirit alone has the power to bring the church to us.

There is, however, one other condition that must be fulfilled: we need to agree on the one object of our pleading, for only when we are united in our asking will the impossible become possible. Unless our prayer is made as one body, the Holy Spirit will not be poured out. Without the pouring out of the Holy Spirit the church will not be established and built up. Without the working of the Holy Spirit there is no perfect fellowship, no living body of Jesus Christ.

The disciples whom Jesus told to wait for the Holy Spirit remained together for days, united in their expectation of God and his power. And when the time was fulfilled the Holy Spirit broke upon them from above, as a wind from heaven, as flames of fire on their heads. They received the gifts of the Holy Spirit and the powers of the world to come. They were united with one another in their teaching, in the breaking of bread, and in the fellowship of the table; they were united in prayer and in the sharing of all their goods. So the church came into being, and so the church will come into being again and again.

But where people do not submit to the working of the Holy Spirit, and where there is not full fellowship of work and goods, nor complete unity and agreement in faith and action, there we cannot speak of the church.

The Spirit of God works everywhere and in all people. God sees this, though it is often hidden from us. For this reason we cannot presume to say where the Holy Spirit is at work. Only God can judge in this way. All the same, there are works, deeds, fruits, results, and effects of the unity of the Spirit that are quite plainly recognizable as coming from the Holy Spirit. About such things we cannot remain silent. Where it is impossible to establish deeds as fruits of the Holy Spirit we may not speak of the church. But where the working of the Holy Spirit is clear, we must for the sake of God's honor say: human beings have not done that; God has done it. There is no other explanation. That is the church.

We confess quite simply that we cannot live in unity for a single day if the Holy Spirit is not given to us again and again. We cannot agree on anything unless Jesus Christ is revealed to us, unless we allow God to work in us and among us. And God works only when we put our own works aside. The mystery of the church is thus deeply related to the mystery of the kingdom of God, for when God reigns, the works of human beings will rest.

Clearly, the mark of the church of God is the laying down of human works. This is of particular significance today, when we stand before the collapse of state and society, when love is growing cold and enmity and hatred are increasing. More than ever before, we must recognize that the church of Jesus Christ is God at work now. And so we must come together to call upon God, despite our smallness, our unworthiness and insufficiency. We must come before God and ask him to pour out upon us that which we do not have, to do among us what we ourselves cannot do. We must ask for the Holy Spirit so that we can live as a witness to the whole world, so that we can become one, even as the Father and Son are one.

—Address, March 1933

•

Arnold's eldest son, Hardy, told of an incident that illustrated his father's emphasis on the work of Jesus as opposed to the work of human beings. It was 1933, shortly after Hitler had come to power; Hardy was studying at Tübingen and had arranged for his father to speak at the Christian Student Union Building. Wanting to secure a good audience, he had plastered the university campus with posters proclaiming a lecture, by Eberhard Arnold, "about the Bruderhof." But his father was indignant; he told his audience that he had come not to talk about the Bruderhof, but about Jesus — and what his life meant at that very grave hour.

•

Jesus — the Jesus distorted by all theological "interpretations" — is practically unknown today. It is high time that he be understood or at the very least be taken seriously. Without rejecting the teachings of Paul, the church which is named after Jesus must turn again to Jesus, as it did in the time of early Christianity, of the Waldensians, and of the Radical Reformation. The church must, at long last, begin again to live according to the four gospels. A life of Christian community can pattern its living only on the words and life of Jesus. There is no one else it can follow.

— Essay, 1934

•

No heights of oratory, no burning enthusiasm could have awakened for Christ the thousands who partook in the united life of the early church. The friends of Jesus knew this very well. Had not the Risen One himself commanded them to wait in Jerusalem for the fulfillment of the great promise? John had baptized in water all those who listened to him. But the first church was to be submerged in the holy wind of Christ's Spirit.

— Essay, 1920

•

At Pentecost, there was such oneness between the apostles and those with them that all those present each heard their own language being spoken. The listening crowd was moved by the same Spirit that overpowered those who spoke. This was neither hypnosis nor human persuasiveness; rather, people allowed God to work in them. They were filled by God's Spirit. And at that very moment the only true collective soul assumed shape and form: the organic unity of the mysterious Body of Christ, the church community, was born.

—Essay, 1920

UNITY

In order to understand Arnold, it is vital to understand what he meant by unity: unity as the hallmark of the church and the sole basis for Christian fellowship. Already in 1913, seven years before he began to live in community, he had concerned himself with the subject.

The church *is* unity: oneness of heart and mind in the Holy Spirit. Whenever this Spirit reveals the will of God, the church is there. Wherever the Spirit brings Christ so near that his word is carried out, the church is there. It is revealed in the united gathering of those to whom Christ has come. It is a gift of his Spirit. Faith in the Holy Spirit must be active as faith in the community of believers, and community can come into being only where Christ comes to each one through his Spirit, touching and filling the inmost heart.

Unless we have surrendered completely to the spirit of unity, we cause division, for we ourselves are emotional and divided people. Separation caused by private life and private property, self-will devoid of love — this is the essence and character of sin. God wills unity and community. God's justice is the love that gathers and unites.

—Essay, 1913

•

Only if we have willing and sincere hearts will we find unanimity in our convictions. We have never found it disturbing when people have come to us representing convictions that differ from ours. On the contrary, that is more fruitful than if we had no chance to hear opposing ideas. All will bring from the storehouse of their earlier convictions those elements that are true, and they will find these again. The more varied our different backgrounds are, the richer the fruits of this diversity will be. But a united conviction can never be produced by forcing anyone to comply. Only the inner persuasion of the Holy Spirit can lead people to true unity.

— Address, May 2, 1933

•

What we have all been looking for is a life where brotherliness is voluntary, where there is no artificial attempt to make people equal, but where all are of equal worth and are therefore free to be very different. The more original an individual is, the better. The greater the differences between people, the closer they can come to each other inwardly. We affirm the individual personality: each person, adult or child, is unique. But this uniqueness, taken to the ultimate depths, must lead us to the church. If we all go into the depths, we will all be united. The more original and genuine we are, the more fully will we all be one.

— Address, July 1935

•

We are not satisfied with intellectual unanimity. It is not enough to set a common goal and use all our willpower to reach it; nor is it enough to vibrate together in an emotional experience. Something quite different has to come over us — something that can lift us above a purely human level.

— Address, March 1932

•

Unity means much more than just mutual good will. It has nothing to do with people's subjective relationships. Rather, it has to do with something much deeper. The spirit of unity is something extremely sober because it is something extremely objective. Even pure rationality will not help us. Rationality is a great gift, but it cannot lead to objective unanimity and solidarity.

Even when something is not completely grasped with the intellect, it is still possible to attain unity of recognition, even in the most difficult matters. It is through inner insight that we come to see a situation as God sees it. And inner insight can be imparted only by the Holy Spirit. It can happen only through the all-seeing Spirit, the Spirit who perceives all things, even those things not understood with the intellect.

Everybody agreeing to make an effort of will is not enough. Everybody having the inner will is not enough. We want to be truly in agreement; no one doubts this will. But the will is not enough. We cannot come to unity by a mere effort of the human will. A different will must triumph over our will. God's will must be revealed.

—Talk, March 1933

•

Arnold insisted that communal living was the only answer to all social, political, and economic problems, but he never held on to his community as its prototype. The following excerpts, from letters to neighboring communities, show his lifelong desire to join hands with others.

It is the age-old curse of Christendom to separate over personal differences, to become divided by ambition, sectarianism, and lack of trust. Instead we should come together. We do not want to put our place or our group in the center. In fact, we need to leave Sannerz, since our work is growing. So we ask you again today that we move together, put all our property together, and become united and unanimous in everything. Of course, this unity will demand a holy and serious struggle.

—Letter to leaders of Neu Sonnefeld, 1925

•

We feel urged to say again: we know that we are united with you all in a lasting, imperishable relationship of brotherhood. We realize that saying this means supporting one another in absolute faithfulness for the life-task given to us both. Our relationship of brotherhood must from now on find its strongest expression in constant mutual service; thus our Sannerz household now stands at your disposal. We are certain that through our daily community of life, work, and goods you will find a second home, and that our community will be encouraged and purified through the task given to you. You will always find our door open, our hands ready — to accept from you and to work for you. Above all, our hearts are open to you, and we want to listen to that which speaks to us through you.

—Letter to group in Wiesbaden, 1927

11

Church and State

THE NEW INCARNATION

In this talk from 1934, Arnold addresses two visitors from England and compares the church, as God's embassy on earth, to the British Embassy in Berlin.

The birth of Jesus shows how every new birth from the Spirit takes place. The word came to Mary. Mary believed. She received the word, the life-giving Spirit. And because she had faith, the living word took flesh and form from her.

Today too the living word wants to take form. Today too the living word wants to become flesh. Today too the eternal Christ wants to have a body. It is for this reason that the Holy Spirit is still sent from the throne of the Father: so that Christ, first embodied as man, might now come into being as the church.

The living word, which is the eternal Christ, became body in Mary's son. And the eternal, living word — Christ — becomes body again in the church. Therefore Paul says that a mystery is entrusted to him, which he calls the mystery of the body of Christ. The fact that the church is the body of Christ means that Christ receives a body, a form or shape, and becomes visible and real in the world. Otherwise the word "body" is meaningless. And when theologians say that what is meant here is the "invisible Christ," they are simply demonstrating the nonsense of which only theologians are capable. The apostles did not believe in ghosts. They spoke either of the completely invisible Spirit or of the body, which is completely visible.

How all of this becomes visible in the church is described further by Paul. He speaks of "the mystery" of the body of Christ, "which is Christ in you"; and then he speaks of the expectation of Christ's future coming, the "hope of glory."

These words have become so trite that they no longer convey anything to us. We have to translate them into the language of today. "Hope" in the New Testament means the expectation, the assurance of a completely new order. "Glory" means the majesty of Christ on his throne. This is the glory: that God now rules over all things, and that Christ rules over all things — that all political, social, educational, and human problems are solved in a concrete way by the rulership of Christ. This is what glory is.

Only very few people in our time grasp this realism of the early Christians. And it is just in this very realistic sense that the word, which is Christ, wants to find a body in the church. Mere words about the future coming of God fade away in people's ears. That is why action is needed. Something must be set up, created, and formed so that no one can pass it by. This is the embodiment, the corporeality.

"Christ in you" is the first part of this mystery. As Christ was in Mary, so Christ is in us who believe and love. Thus we live in accordance with the future; the character of our conduct is the character of God's future. This is not something moralistic or legalistic; it is something very natural and simple. It takes place now, through Christ in the church. The future kingdom takes on a physical form in the church.

Just for this reason, the church must demonstrate perfect peace and perfect justice. This is why it cannot shed blood or tolerate private property. This is why it cannot lie or take an oath. This is why it cannot tolerate the destruction of bridal purity and of faithfulness in marriage. This is why it must also be free of the actions by which individual people make themselves great. None of us must think that we are a second or third or fourth Christ.

The church as a body, and not the individual within the church, is the incarnation of Christ.

Everything about this church should be in keeping with the simplicity of Jesus. Poverty, too, belongs to this embodiment: because we who represent the church are called to serve the whole world and because there is so much need in the world, we must live as simply as possible in order to help as many people as possible. But it is an error to mix this specific task of the church with public affairs. Paul shows clearly that the unique task of the church is to be the embodiment of Christ, thrust in among the nations.

It is not the task of this body of Christ to attain a political voice. According to the apostolic truth there is no such thing as a Christian state. A Christian church does not fight for the interests of the state. Nor does the church fight against the interests of the state. There is no such thing as Christian politics in the League of Nations. No head of a state can wield the sword in the name of Christ. No church can say that it agrees to this. Nor can a League of Nations arm and organize a punitive police force in the name of Christ.

A Christian is not active in politics. The apostle Paul says we are ambassadors of the kingdom of God. And the kingdom of God is not represented by any state of this world, but by the church. This means that we ought to do nothing at all other than what God himself would do for his kingdom. Just as the British ambassador in Berlin does nothing other than the will of his superiors in London, so we too must do the will of God alone. We are no longer subject to the laws of this world; the grounds of our embassy are inviolable, just as in the residence of an ambassador, only the laws of the country that ambassador represents are valid. The will of God is to unite, and thus our task is to reconcile and to unite. We have no other mission in this world.

When we take this task upon ourselves we enter into mortal danger. For whoever goes the way of Christ goes the way of the cross; world, state, and society are not willing to follow his call. Nevertheless, there is certainty in the depths of every human heart that his way is the way of truth, and this gives us the courage to speak. There is no greater bravery than that of faith. There is no greater courage than that of love.

— Address, August 1934

CHURCH AND STATE

From the moment Adolf Hitler was appointed Reich Chancellor, Arnold voiced grave concern over Germany's future. But his belief in the ultimate evil of the state came long before the Nazis' ascent to power; in fact, he had come to this conviction two decades earlier, after the First World War. The following address was delivered in Liechtenstein in 1934. Despite the relative advantage of this location, Arnold's boldness is remarkable; he was still a German citizen, and the rash of murders and "suicides" among radicals and nonconformists back home had already begun.

No absolute monarchy in the past ever achieved the centralization seen today in our fascist state and in Bolshevism. Just as the monarch is meant to represent the whole state, so too, present-day centralism — as in the case of Mussolini and Hitler — combines everything in one person. It is like Rome under the emperors.

No emperor, however, ever claimed the kind of self-deification these men claim today. The Romans did set up small incense altars for Nero and other emperors, altars at which incense was offered in testimony of the religious significance of a unified emperorship. But the sacrifice was made to the "genius" of the emperor, and not to the emperor personally. Neither Nero nor any other emperor ever managed to have the Romans call out "Heil Nero!" from every street corner.

The present-day dictator has been so utterly abandoned by what is spiritual that he does not even believe in the genius of his dictatorship, but only in his own small person. Thus idolatry is coarsened in the most vulgar way. What people worship nowadays is the tone of voice and the hair and the nose of the dictator. The human person has been made into an idol. What the dictator says gets done. Thinking is forbidden.

This modern fascism is a phenomenon that makes me feel like weeping day and night. Goebbels says, "If we are right, it follows that no one else is right. For us there is no justice other than self-interest." So there is no justice whatever; objective justice is eliminated, and stupidity reigns. In the twentieth century, that is shattering. I don't believe that such a destructive spirit ever prevailed among the early Germanic tribes. Their chiefs were bound by the decision of the council meeting and to the concept of justice for the tribe as a whole. But what we have today is egoism and self-assertion beyond all law and all thought. Who still believes in progress today?

What power opposes this force? What is England's parliamentary monarchy doing? What are the other states with great spiritual traditions doing? Where are the churches, with their theologians and philosophers? There have been raids on the Bishop's Palace. Catholic priests have been arrested and taken to concentration camps. Two of the most outstanding priests have been murdered. And yet none of this prevents the pope from dealing with Hitler again and again.

The Evangelicals are led by a cleric with an ignorance unprecedented in thousands of years. The Reform Church of Zwingli and Calvin has proven more capable of resistance than the Lutheran Church; Orthodox Protestant groups have bristled a little, most vigorously in the Rhineland and Württemberg, where pietism and the personal experience of salvation have been the strongest. But it seems that one established church after another is succumbing to brutal violence and base deceit.

The Confessing Church Synods have given the word: "No withdrawing from the church!" But that cripples every bit of initiative. For if the established church is godless, if it is ruled by demons and idolatry, it is useless to say, "We protest, but we remain in the church." The reason for this limp attitude is clear. Even protesting groups in the Catholic and Protestant churches render unconditional homage to the National Socialist state. They give the *Heil Hitler* salute. They are willing to take active part in government functions. So what good is it if, from within the churches, they protest isolated incidents that lead to suppression of free speech, brutal murder, and all manner of other horrors, while at the same time supporting the overall application of this evil system?

The failure of the churches of the Reformation to take a radical, early Christian position with regard to state and society is taking its toll. We are paying here for the historical sins of the Peasants' War: the bondage to the rule of princes and the outrages committed against the popular Anabaptist Movement. We are reminded of the way Christianity in England sold out to the state in Oliver Cromwell's time and afterward.

The cause of this error lies in a misunderstanding of Paul's words in Romans 13, "Let each person be subject to the governing authorities." Verses 1–5 are quoted repeatedly by the established churches to defend their interests in the state. These verses show what the state's task is: to punish evil with the sword.

In contrast to this, Paul gives the answer of love, in verses 8–10. "Love is the fulfilling of the law," and "Owe no one anything, except to love one another." Paul says that the Christian way is different from that of the state.

There is no state that does not have a police force, which maintains order with the sword. This is what God has ordained in an unchristian world so that evil does not gain the upper hand: child molesters, for example, simply cannot be allowed to run free. We cannot stand up in London and preach, "Away with all policemen!" We cannot deny the necessity of government order for the world of evil.

But the Christian church is in a different region, the region of absolute love. Here there is no police system. The church will suffer death at the hands of the state, but it will not partake in evil. For this reason the church cannot deliver up a criminal. It simply cannot.

There are two worlds, then. One is the world of evil; the other is the world of pure light and pure love, which has nothing to do with violence.

•

Our own love of Jesus can never be what is most important. What is far more crucial is that God and God's kingdom prevail among us in such a way that we represent its cause in the face of all other circumstances, conditions, and relationships. As a result, we will find ourselves to be in decisive opposition to the world around us. This includes opposition to the state, which has to defend private property and which is maintained by force and by violence.

We respect government as God-ordained. But we are called to an order of society utterly different from the state and the present social order. That is why we refuse to swear oaths before any court of law; why we refuse to serve in any state as soldiers or police officers; why we refuse to serve in any important government post. For all of these are connected with law courts, the police, or the military.

We oppose outright the present order of society. We represent a different order: that of the communal church as it was in Jerusalem after the pouring out of the Holy Spirit. There, the multitude of believers became one heart and one soul. On the social level, their oneness was visible in perfect brotherliness. On the economic level, they lived in complete community of goods, free from all private property and from any compulsion. And we are called to represent the same life in the world today. Of course, we cannot put this burden on others, unless they prize the greatness of God's kingdom above everything else and are certain that there is no other way to go.

—Talk, March 1933

•

The first Christians expected human beings to be freed from suffering, to be liberated from injustice, war, and bloodshed. They expected the transformation of all things political and economic, resulting in new relationships of unadulterated justice and love. Therefore it is correct, to a certain extent, to compare the socialist expectation of a future state to the early Christian hope for God's kingdom. Yet there is an important difference: the socialist ideal arises from a purely economic concept of history.

This stands in sharp contrast to the basic truth of Christianity, in which the spirit, as the highest and greatest manifestation of life, rules over matter.

Still, the material world is not foreign to God. God is a God of Life, and God encompasses and commands all life even in its primitive and degenerate forms. This includes matter. Only the perverse idealism of false Christianity teaches that the world of matter and the senses is unspiritual and therefore to be despised. Only those without love or spirit or power try to appease suffering humankind with promises of the life beyond. This is why the socialists revolt in the name of materialism; they oppose religious idealism because they recognize the ethical demands of the spirit within the material sphere and seek to fulfill them in this sphere. Even though they put aside the spirit, their materialistic interpretation of history is better than a high-flown Christian spirituality that simply accepts the injustice of the world as it is.

Of course, the socialist revolution can never be confused with a spiritual awakening. One need not even mention the sewers of human weakness, the whirlpools of animal blood-thirst, the bottomless abyss of petty egoism, and the demonic thirst for power present in the socialist wave — things all found in people who call themselves Christians as well. Yet no one can deny that the attack of socialism against the present social order is a challenge to our consciences and reminds us more strongly than any sermon that our task is to live in active protest against everything that opposes God's will. We who call ourselves Christians have done so little in this regard that we must ask, Are we really Christians at all?

A Christian church as such is not called to abolish the existing state order; the power of the state and its juridical order are instruments of God, needed to hold murder and hatred, lying and deceit, injustice and impurity at bay. But determined Christians cannot be undiscriminating in their dealings with the state. Their consciences will rise up against any government that acts as executioner in the employ of the rich, just as they will protest the rapacious egoism of the proletariat. And in the conflict between individual and collective will, between individuality and communality, Christians must take the side of the social spirit of fellowship and community.

Plato, Aristotle, and Hegel held the task of the state to be that of realizing justice and virtue. But one thing they did not see: that force and violence must ultimately fail. And the state lives exclusively in the sphere of force. Socialism, with its rigorous organization of the masses and strictly applied discipline, is simply another form of totalitarian militarism. Marxism, too, has to compensate for the absence of the Spirit by applying coercive measures. Therefore the dedicated church can have nothing to do with these powers of the state.

The church represents one thing alone: the all-sustaining power of love. It is the church's task to exert its influence on the political life for the sake of social justice and peace, for the sake of encompassing love. But to master the murderous spirit of mammon, the church must call on spiritual forces far greater than the ideals of economic politics. It has the one and only hope by which to achieve unity and freedom among human beings: the one spirit who is the Spirit of God.

— Essay, 1919

12

Expectation

Arnold's faith was in the future, yet he lived fully in the present. Even after the rise of Nazism had forced the Bruderhof to send its young men and children abroad, he pressed forward with plans to expand the buildings and business operations at the Rhön Bruderhof in Germany. He liked to quote Martin Luther: "If I knew the world would end tomorrow, I would still plant my apple tree today."

Faith in God means faith for the future. Those who live in God do not look back, but forward. Those who are alive do not look back over the short span of their own lives, nor even over the greater span of religious development, to find a past realization of their current longing. They look forward into time, toward the goal, toward the destiny of humankind as it should be and as it shall be.

When we put our hand to God's plow, we look forward; our lives are directed by the future. But if we lose ourselves in historical speculation and self-absorbed reveries, we are not fit for God's kingdom. Certainly, our faith today is linked to God's working in the past, for God is the same yesterday, today, and forever. But a pietism that immerses itself in the Bible only to gain insights into religious history is a weak and poor thing, because it stands in opposition to the almighty, all-embracing, creative God. There is, however, a meditation on scripture that can lift us beyond our small ego and our petty affairs, a meditation that carries us into God's heart, so that we may take part already now in God's all-embracing kingdom.

But our expectation of this kingdom cannot be a passive waiting, a sweet, soft preoccupation with ourselves and our like-minded friends. No, if we truly expect God's kingdom we will be filled with divine power. Then the social justice of the future, with its purity of heart and divine fellowship, will be realized now, wherever Jesus himself is present. Our belief in the future must bring change to the present!

The spirit of expectation is the spirit of action because it is the spirit of faith. Faith is bravery. Faith is reality. If we have faith, even only a small seed, we cannot regard anything as impossible. For faith is what gives us a clear picture of life's ultimate powers. It discloses God's heart to us as the pulse of the entire living creation and shows us that the secret of life is love.

If we live in love we can never exhaust ourselves in psychic introspection or in narrow conventionality. If we are gripped by the experiences of faith and of love, by the expectation of Christ and his second coming, we will act. For God's love is boundless; it applies to public life just as much as to the individual heart, to economic as well as political affairs.

If we expect God we will be purified by the purity of the One we expect. There is nothing that heightens the conscience more than such expectation; it eliminates all relativity and overcomes weak submission to the status quo. It enables us to live so securely in the future world that we as its heralds dare, here and now, to assume the unbroken, unconditional character of the kingdom.

Our expectation of the future must mean certainty that the divine will conquer the demonic, that love will conquer hate, that the all-embracing will conquer the isolated. And certainty tolerates no limitation. God embraces everything. When we trust in God for the future, we trust for the present. When we have innermost faith in God, this faith will prove valid for all areas of life.

—Essay, 1920

NOW IS THE TIME

In this talk, Arnold exhorts his listeners to make their lives count. He foresees an awakening of the masses that will stretch far beyond the personal to encompass and transform all of society, and challenges those who call themselves believers to make this happen. Such an awakening will not come about without struggle and sacrifice, but anything less would not be worthy of God's great calling.

All the various movements of the past decades will one day converge in a radical awakening of the masses that leads the way to social justice and to God's unity, that is to say, to the church, to the kingdom of God, and to community in action. We must set our little Bruderhof in the midst of this mighty task and sacrifice ourselves. We must not cling to a time when we were (or still are) a small circle of people knowing each other intimately. Rather we must be ready to be consumed in a mighty outpouring of the Holy Spirit, to be merged with it completely.

What we need now is mission. Mission means reaching the millions who live in cities, the hundreds of thousands in industrial centers, the tens of thousands in medium-sized towns, the thousands in small towns, and the hundreds in villages — all these at once. Like a volcanic eruption, a spiritual revolution needs to spread through the country, to spur people to crucial decisions. People have to recognize the futility of splitting life up into politics, economics, the humanities, and religion. We must be awakened to a life in which all of these things are completely integrated.

We need to find an attitude of responsibility for public affairs, and this attitude must be completely practical, completely spiritual, and thoroughly believing. We must gain an inner understanding and a broad view of how all things affect each other and through this find the right way to tackle all kinds of social problems. With this understanding we will be able to work creatively in the economic sphere. We will do all this in faith, and this faith will find its fulfillment in the love that creates community in all things.

So we must win a faith that does not break down in the face of social ills but that completely envelopes and transforms them, a faith that embraces economic problems and solves them. This means a faith that takes on all inner and outer tasks and makes them part of our daily life; it means faith in a God who created everything and provides for everything and who does not let go of any part of his will.

The new awakening must therefore be both religious and social, a Christ-centered communist awakening, an awakening to God's kingdom, to grace as a reality. This is the only kind of awakening that comes into question.

But it will be paid for with bitterest pain. The suffering of Jesus, which he experienced to the full for the sake of this future joy, will be our suffering. We shall be persecuted to death with hatred and scorn from all sides, in particular by the most religious, the most respectable and cultivated people. They will slander us and send us to psychiatrists. The police and the military will be called out against us. All sorts of lawsuits will be brought against us in the courts. An economic boycott will be started against us, and attempts will be made to drive us out of the country by taking away our livelihood. Ultimately they will pass special laws against us, as they once did to the Socialists and the Jesuits.

When the movement has reached its peak, it will be so dangerous that capitalism will see itself imperiled by it. Wealthy landowners will see it as a threat to their position, and the state will see its existence endangered — for where shall the state get its income if its members live in absolute propertylessness? It will foresee its own dissolution and so will have to call in the executioners.

This image of the future appears fantastic only to the unbelieving. The believer who reckons with the historical realities of Jesus' time and of the Reformation will feel that all this must surely take place, and very soon at that. But if we are as convinced of the truth as we have often asserted, then we must live in such a way that all this can really happen. More than anything else we must arrive at such a reverence for the working of the

Holy Spirit that our trivial concerns over personal matters — the state of our health and our emotional needs — are sacrificed in this mighty flame.

Everything will depend on whether or not the last hour finds us a generation worthy of greatness. And the only thing worthy of God's greatness is our readiness to die for his cause. So we must show this readiness to die in the trivial details of daily life, or we will not be able to stand firm in the critical hour to come. We need to overcome completely all petty points of view, all purely personal opinions and feelings, all fear, care, and inner uncertainty — in short, all unbelief. In its place we must put faith, faith which is as small as a seed but which has the power to grow.

This faith is active in our midst, through Christ and the Holy Spirit. We have sensed it, but we have not lived according to it. If the Holy Spirit has withdrawn from us, it is because we have grieved him and driven him away, because we have given him little regard and no reverence, and have esteemed our own affairs more than his. Then all we can do is to ask for judgment, and to believe that this judgment will prepare us at long last for mission, that we may be freed and released from all that comes from ourselves. Only then will we be usable for God's will.

Whether the twentieth century is shattered for God's kingdom or simply passes by depends in part on us. We know what is at stake; we know the will of God. We have felt the power of the Holy Spirit and the powers of the future world. So let us get going; now is the time!

— Address, August 1928

•

The whole world is shaking at its joints. We have the frightening impression that we stand before a great and catastrophic judgment. If this catastrophe does not take place, it is only because it has been averted by God's direct intervention. And the church is called to move God — yes, God himself — to act. This does not mean that God will not or cannot act unless we ask him, but rather that he waits for people to believe in him and expect his intervention. For God acts among us only to the extent that we ask for his action and accept it with our hearts and lives. This is the secret of God's intervention in history.

The nineteenth-century German pastor Blumhardt says that God waits for breaches to be made by human beings. And just as in each person there is a small window through which the light of God can shine, so it is with nations. The great majority of people do not open themselves up to the greatness of God. In their self-willed impertinence they hold up their own actions instead of God's. But wherever people are fully united in their waiting for God, there God intervenes — in the history of the nations and of humanity. No one can escape this reality. Even governments cannot completely evade the intervention of God.

Before the Holy Spirit was poured out, the disciples had to wait for God's kingdom to break in. They knew that the first sign of God's kingdom would be a blowing wind, the rushing breath of the Holy Spirit. This wind came just like the wind that comes before a thunderstorm: a roaring wind that breaks the calm and announces its presence to all. And the wind that comes before a storm is part of that storm. Thus it is clear that the experience of the Holy Spirit can never be a merely personal matter. It can never be private or subjective. No, the Holy Spirit is the voice of God that precedes the day of judgment and the day of redemption. It is the wind that heralds the breaking in of God's kingdom over all people and all nations.

This is how the disciples in Jerusalem understood it. And it is what we must now expect, for the whole of humanity — for all peoples and nations, for all cities and villages, for the billions of people inhabiting the earth. We expect it not only for those people who are living now but also for all those who have died and who are not yet born.

Jesus said, "Until now you have asked nothing in my name; now ask in my name, and nothing will be impossible for you. You will move mountains and uproot trees; everything you ask will be given to you if you ask in my name." So we ask now for each of us and for the whole world that the new day dawn through the pouring out of the Holy Spirit, that the heavens be opened, that they come down to us in flames of the Holy Spirit.

Then the whole earth will be filled with the Spirit, and there will be no laws. For the knowledge of God will be poured out over all the lands, like water covering the whole earth. Just this is the mystery of the new kingdom: that the Spirit of God, the sap of the tree, the blood of the Son, will fill and penetrate all. There will be no need for commandments and prohibitions, for tables and tablets. In this kingdom everything will be ordered through the inner birth and inspiration which come from the rulership of the Spirit.

—Address, September 1935

For Further Reading

The following titles by and about Eberhard Arnold are available exclusively from The Plough Publishing House, Farmington, PA 15437; Tel.: 800-521-8011.

The Early Christians

This collection of primary sources includes first-hand accounts of life in the early church by Origen, Tertullian, Polycarp, Clement of Alexandria, Irenaeus, and others, as well as equally revealing material from their pagan critics and persecutors. Historical and contextual notes support each entry, but this is no dry, scholarly book: Arnold's selections, ranging from apologies and confessions of faith to short sayings, parables, and poetry, are pithy and eminently readable.

Innerland

Arnold's *magnum opus*, this book absorbed his energies off and on from 1916, when he published the first chapter, to 1935, the last year of his life. Packed in metal boxes and buried at night for safekeeping from the Nazis, who raided the author's study a year before his death, *Innerland* attacks the spirits that not only animated Nazi Germany in the 1930s, but still animate our own society today. A wellspring of spiritual depth, it invites readers to turn from the chaos of a life distracted by violence and greed to that "inner land of the invisible" where we will find strength and peace.

Salt and Light

A collection of short talks and essays on the Sermon on the Mount calling us to obedience and repentance: to the overturning of the old and the building up of the new. Arnold's enthusiasm leaves no room for scholarly analysis; instead, his words are simple, direct, and radiant.

Why We Live in Community

This new edition of Arnold's best-known essay now appears with two interpretive talks by Thomas Merton, given at the Monastery of the Precious Blood in Eagle River, Alaska, in September 1968. A "must read" for any serious Christian.

God's Revolution

This anthology of selections from Arnold's writings (arranged by topic) challenges readers to break from the stifling complacency of conventional life. But be warned: Arnold sees discipleship not as the quiet road to religious fulfillment, but as revolution — a transformation that begins within but eventually permeates and transforms even the outer aspects of life. Here is the raw reality of the gospel that has the power to change the world.

The Individual and World Need

One of Arnold's most compelling works, this essay explores the relationship of the individual to world sin and suffering and directs us to a solution. Enlivened by anecdotal illustrations ranging from the ancient myth of Prometheus to the expressionist Franz Werfel, Arnold's message is simple but revolutionary: only by overcoming isolation and individualism will we ever overcome the suffering of the world and enter into a life of unity and love.

Eberhard Arnold: A Testimony to Church Community from His Life and Writings

For a concise, readable introduction to Arnold's writings, this is a good place to start. It contains a biographical sketch, selections from his most important works, and brief memoirs by friends and colleagues.

Against the Wind

In this new biography, Markus Baum recounts Arnold's renunciation of private property, nationalism, and military service, his abhorrence of conventional piety, and his love for the early church fathers. Most of all, it gives flesh, blood, and personality to a man whose unwavering conviction and contagious faith earned him hatred as well as admiration.

A Joyful Pilgrimage: My Life in Community

Emmy Arnold was already in her seventies when she began to write down her story, but the details she recounts were as alive for her then as if they had happened the day before. But this book, by Arnold's widow, is animated neither by nostalgia nor sentimental yearnings. Rather, it is driven by a vision of a society built on justice and love, and by an expectant longing for God's coming kingdom.